OLIVIER

OLIVIER

edited by
Logan Gourlay

Weidenfeld and Nicolson
London

Printed in Great Britain by
Bristol Typesetting Co Ltd
Barton Manor St Philips Bristol

Contents

Illustrations

31 As Shylock in *The Merchant of Venice*.
32 As James Tyrone in *Long Day's Journey into Night*.
33 As Andrew Wyke in *Sleuth*.
34 With Kenneth Tynan.

Acknowledgements

I am indebted of course to all those who have contributed to this book by giving me interviews or by writing their own impressions, and trusting them to my editorship. I owe a special debt of gratitude to Sir John Gielgud, Sir Alec Guinness, Sir Michael Redgrave and Douglas Fairbanks Jr, who were most co-operative in difficult circumstances.

I must thank Angus McBean in particular who gave me his written views and also loaned me a selection from his unique collection of photographs of Lord Olivier, which is now in the Harvard College Library.

Sir Noël Coward and Max Adrian died while this book was in preparation and to the many tributes already paid to them I should like to add mine in appreciation of their invaluable advice, and of their unquenchable humour.

I should mention that I have been collecting material for this book over a period of more than three years and a few minor details in some of the contributions may have been altered and out-dated by recent events and changes in administration at the National Theatre. In these cases I have not altered the text.

The newspapers and magazines, which have provided me with background information, are too numerous to list here. I am grateful to Studio Vista Ltd for permission to quote from *In Various Directions* by Tyrone Guthrie. Of the many books I have read and consulted the most valuable have been *The Oliviers* by Felix Barker (1953), *Othello, The National Theatre Production*, edited by Kenneth Tynan (1966), *Laurence Olivier* (Great Contemporaries) by W. A. Darlington (1968), *Actors on Acting*, edited by Toby Cole and Helen Krich Chonoy (1970, USA), *The Player Kings* by Richard Findlater (1971), *The Modern Actor* by Michael Billington (1973) and *Playback* by Ronald Hayman (1973).

Without the guidance and encouragement of my literary agent, Jonathan Clowes, and without the interest and support of Tony Godwin at Weidenfeld and Nicolson, this book would not have been possible. An added word of thanks to Mark Amory at Weidenfeld and Nicolson for his editorial co-operation and understanding.

Among those who have done any research work on my behalf, Anne Cunningham deserves my special thanks for her helpfulness and accuracy.

Finally I must offer my personal thanks to my wife, who has patiently and helpfully listened to more discussion about Lord Olivier and his work than any woman should who is not (a) playing opposite him, or (b) married to him.

Introduction

Laurence Olivier has been a professional actor for over fifty years, and for at least the past two decades he has been generally regarded as the greatest living actor in the English-speaking world, yet very few books have been written about him and his remarkable career. This is partly due to the man himself and to the reticent part of his complex character, which makes him at times leap defensively out of the limelight, actively discouraging prospective biographers and chroniclers of his doings.

He has let it be known of late that he intends to write his auto-biography and when he does it should make a fascinating volume, or volumes. But until they appear, or until the appearance of an up-to-date authorized biography, I make no apologies for offering this book. It makes no claims to be a definitive biographical work, but I hope it throws some light on the man, and particularly on the actor, by presenting him as seen through the eyes of colleagues and friends.

While I cannot resist quoting the perhaps over-quoted words of Robert Burns 'Oh, wad some Pow'r the giftie gie us, To see our-selves as ithers see us!', it would be presumptuous of me to suggest that this book bestows any gift on Lord Olivier.

However when he comes to write his autobiography he may find it of some help to know the views and assessments of the 'ithers' I have collected here. They do not cover every aspect of his life and times, but they are representative of the principal periods of his career. Although nothing approximating to a complete portrait can be presented in this framework some of the key areas of the canvas are sketched in; and there is some indication from close observers of the location of the warts, which can of course be diffi-cult to place accurately, particularly when a self-portrait is tackled.

A greater difficulty in any kind of biographical study of a living person is avoiding an excess of over-respectful, laudatory, rose pinks; and when the subject belongs to the highly-coloured world of the theatre, and when he is a legend in his own lifetime, the difficulty is greatly increased.

At the same time, while avoiding the boring and sickly hues of homage, it is essential that due prominence is given to his outstanding, imperishable achievements as an actor.

In this context the question that inescapably crops up is what has been his greatest performance? And the answer invariably is that from such an abundance of acting excellence it is impossible to choose one performance in preference to all the others. However a consensus does seem to emerge from the opinions in the following pages, and it is that one of his truly great, if not the greatest, performances began on the opening night of *Richard* III at the New Theatre in London in 1944, when he limped slowly downstage to begin the soliloquy:

'Now is the winter of our discontent
Made glorious summer by this son of York . . .'

Yet during rehearsals he had been full of self-doubts and for the first time in his career he had found it difficult to learn his lines. In his well-documented biography, *The Oliviers*, Felix Barker reports: 'On the night before the opening Olivier was up until 4 a.m. in a room at Claridge's going over and over his part while Vivien Leigh and an old friend Garson Kanin, the American producer, gave him the cues.'

Another old friend, John Mills, has a story which illustrates that Olivier's fears and forebodings had reached a neurotic pitch just before the curtain went up. When Mills was getting ready to go to the first night he received a phone call from Olivier asking him to come round to the dressing-room before the performance.

Mills arrived to find Olivier pacing up and down the dressing room in costume and fully made-up as Richard. He stared down the long, dagger-like, nose at Mills, fixed him with a piercing eye and opened the thin slit of a mouth to say: 'You are about to see the worst performance I've ever given. I haven't even been able to learn the bloody lines. I'll be terrible, terrible. I want you to know as one of my old friends. You can tell any of my other friends who're out there to expect the worst. If you're all warned in advance you won't be too disappointed.'

Mills, who had never seen him so deeply sunk in despondency tried to humour him, but it was useless. Now, full of foreboding himself, he went to the front of the house to await disaster. Then, as we know now, the curtain rose on a performance of such trans-cendent quality it will never be forgotten by those who were privileged to see it.

The pre-curtain moments of self-laceration were never again mentioned by Olivier to Mills. However there can be no doubt that the fears were very real and much in excess of the usual first-night nerves. They may have been related to an instinctive assump-tion of the tortured, sado-masochistic character of Richard. What-ever the cause it is interesting to speculate as to whether the heights of achievement he reached that night were in inverse ratio to the depths of self-doubt he touched before the performance.

His attitude was very different on another occasion involving John Mills. After a long spell in the film studios Mills was appre-hensively preparing for a return to the stage in *Ross*, the Terence Rattigan play about T. E. Lawrence. Mills had been persuaded to do it by Olivier who had warned him of the dangers of staying off the stage for too long a period, and it was to Olivier that he turned for help, especially about the conquering of first-night nerves. Olivier told him, 'There's a trick I've used on occasions and I find it works. Try it. Go to the theatre early on the first night, and get made up well in advance of the curtain. Then walk on to the stage and imagine that the curtain is already up and that you are facing the audience. Look out at them and shout, "You are about to see the greatest fucking performance of your entire theatre-going lives. And I will be giving it. You lucky people."

'Tell them that once or twice. Then go back to your dressing room and relax, and you'll find that when the curtain does go up you'll have the necessary confidence.'

Somewhere between that attitude to his work and his feelings on the first night of *Richard* III is the balance Olivier has sought throughout his career. In a BBC interview with Ken Tynan Olivier said : 'I think the most difficult equation to solve is the union of the two things that are absolutely necessary to an actor. One is confidence, absolute confidence, and the other an equal amount of humility toward the work. That's a very hard equation.'

In that same interview he talked about a remark he once made to the effect that 'you need to be a bit of a bastard to be a star'.

'I think that came out of the fact that at one time I may have thought that somebody lacked the necessary *edge* to be a star. I think you've got to have a certain edge that might be traced to being a bit of a bastard, inside. You've got to be a bit of a bastard

to understand bastards, and you've got to understand everybody . . .'

As Harry Andrews and others indicate in the following pages,
Olivier has on occasions made decisions, involving colleagues and
in pursuit of his aims and ambitions, that could be called self-
centred and even ruthless : the *edge* has cut when necessary.

However the fact remains that not a great deal is known about
Olivier off stage, even backstage. In his valuable book *The Player
Kings* Richard Findlater writes : '. . . a man hailed as the greatest
actor in the world has the air on managerial duty, of an eminently
successful and unstuffy City executive or solicitor . . .'

William Gaskill talks about Olivier's chameleon-like abilities and
it may be that he adopts the solicitor/businessman's grey-and-black
pin stripes as protective colouring against an over-curious public,
prying press and meddlesome friends. Even his wife Joan Plowright
has referred to his 'unapproachability'. John Osborne points out
that Olivier is an elusive and complex man, who defies analysis as
most highly talented men do; and in the words of Michael Redgrave
he can only be summed up 'in a series of contradictions'.

Olivier himself in a self-obfuscating mood has said 'I'm not sure
what I'm like and I'm not sure I want to know', but he also made
one definitive, unassailable statement, 'I believe I was born to be
an actor'. Yet the odds appeared to be against that possibility at
his birth on 22 May 1907 in Dorking, Surrey. His father was a
High Anglican churchman of Huguenot origin, and for five generations the male Oliviers had gone into the pulpit. However at the
age of 16 when he was thinking about following his elder brother,
who had gone to India to work on a plantation, he was astonished
to be told by his father, 'Don't be a fool – you're going on the
stage'.

A year later he was enrolled as a bursary student at the Central
School of Speech and Drama by the principal Elsie Fogerty, and
Olivier likes to claim that his well-known obsession with make-up
can be traced to the fact that at their first interview she pointed
to his forehead and told him he had a weakness there. Whenever
possible he has hidden behind false noses and under heavy wigs,
and it is ironical that the man, who was dismissed by the critics
after his first Romeo as not much more than a good-looking mati-
nee idol, and who was publicized by Hollywood after his success
in *Wuthering Heights* as a new 'romantic profile', has never considered himself specially handsome; it is no doubt significant in

terms of his development as a serious actor that he never took the critics or the publicists too seriously.

Among the men whom Olivier did take seriously in his early career, and who greatly influenced him, were Barry Jackson, who ran the Birmingham rep theatre where Olivier spent two formative years learning his craft in the 1920s, and Noël Coward, who after Olivier had been in a series of about half a dozen flops in the West End, advised him to take a dullish part in a new play Coward had written – 'You'd better be in a success for a change'. Reluctantly Olivier agreed to play Victor Prynne in *Private Lives*.

A few years later Coward made Olivier another offer he was reluctant to accept. It was to play the part based on the tempestuous John Barrymore in a play called *Theatre Royal*, but the snag was that the engagement would be for only two weeks on tour, and Brian Aherne would take over when the play came to London. Olivier thought about it carefully and made his decision : he would accept and he would play the part with such brilliance and panache that Aherne would think twice about trying to follow him. Olivier's plan worked, for Aherne suddenly decided he should accept an offer to appear in New York, and Olivier triumphed in London with an energetic, exhibitionist performance. However, he became over-energetic one night, misjudged a leap from a balcony and broke his ankle.

That leap was one of the first of those acrobatic bits of business which have characterized his performances, and the whole *Theatre Royal* episode reveals another related, Olivierean, characteristic. It is his boldness, his creative enterprise and energy, his willingness, in his own unpretentious words, 'to have a bash'. John Gielgud in the interview I quote in this book refers to the way he 'dashes with a part and really wrings its neck. . . .'

Throughout his professional life when faced with a decision, not only about the interpretation of a part, but the general direction of his career he has chosen the adventurous, hazardous path rather than the safe, conformist and comfortable one. His gambles have not always come off, but it is his eagerness to experiment, to meet, and even create challenges which has helped to sustain and renew him from decade to decade.

When he first went to the Old Vic in 1937 to tackle a full-length *Hamlet* under the direction of Tyrone Guthrie he had to overcome an atmosphere of antipathy from the theatre's regulars, who regarded him as an inexperienced interloper from the West End.

When he presented an elaborate production of *Romeo and Juliet* on Broadway in 1940 with Vivien Leigh, he backed it with £12,000 of their own hard-earned Hollywood money, and lost every penny.

When he presented his compelling *Oedipus* at the Old Vic in 1945, he startled the critics and the first-night audience by bringing the curtain down with a strikingly contrasted comic portrayal of Mr Puff in *The Critic*.

When he decided to play the part of Archie Rice, a shabby, end-of-the-pier comic, in *The Entertainer* at the Royal Court in 1957, he defied the counsel of his friends and associates, who warned him that he was risking his established reputation in a sordid piece by John Osborne whom they regarded as an untried, jumped-up, playwright; but the result was a performance that is regarded as his greatest outside the classics (and by William Gaskill, for example, as his greatest performance in any play).

When he presented his negroid Othello at the National in 1964, John Osborne and others found it 'unspeakably vulgar', but Franco Zeffirelli said 'it's grand and majestic'; and obviously the black boldness of Olivier's interpretation will keep the argument and discussion going until the historians take over.

So the Olivierean effrontery, what the Jews would call, untranslatably, his *chutzpah*, and what today's youth would define as his 'cool', has never deserted him, and hopefully never will.

What, apart from the *chutzpah*, are the other main qualities of his acting? What are the highest common denominators? His range is so wide, his mimetic talents so developed, that they are not easy to list. But of course there are characteristics common to all his work and it is possible to attempt to define the quintessential Olivierean performance.

That omnipresent audacity will manifest itself physically, if in no other way. He will execute a leap or fall worthy of a circus performer in its daring and dexterity as he did in *Coriolanus*; or he will perform a little dance like his *Schadenfreude* skip in *The Merchant of Venice* when he heard of the loss of Antonio's ships; or he will utter a howl of anguish as he did in *Oedipus* that echoes in the mind's ear for ever after as the uttermost expression of human misery and tragedy. His make-up of course, including, if the part allows, a peninsula of a nose, will be abundantly and heavily evident. His voice will not only be clearly audible at the back of the gallery but will have the power of a tocsin to summon an audience back from the bars; and his eyes will penetrate the darkness with mesmeric power.

The unmistakable minor effects will be there – the arresting lift of the voice at the end of a line; the pointing of the index finger in a minatory gesture when the hand is a pistol, and the upturning of the palms when the hands are eloquent saucers, petitioning for the alms of understanding and sympathy.

The whole performance, every speech and movement, will have a studied, unifying rhythm and behind it there will be the suggestion of a primitive beat, threatening danger; and, though the theme be tragic, it will be underscored with a sharp, mordant and unexpected humour. Above all the performance will have a throbbing vitality that will always seem to be held partly in check, and a sexuality, which every member of the audience will sense (and which Margaret Leighton admits she could feel at the other side of the Old Vic stage). Yet there will be at least one moment when a small gesture, a tilt of the head, or an arching of the eyebrow, will be essentially feminine in its grace and subtlety.

Michael Billington in his perceptive book *The Modern Actor* writes about 'the androgynous bisexual quality that invariably underpins great acting ... Amongst male performers I can think of no one who makes more positive and creative use of his femininity than Laurence Olivier.'

Ken Tynan in the book about the National Theatre *Othello* tells a story about Elia Kazan saying the adjective he would use to sum up Olivier would be 'girlish' meaning that 'he's coy, he's vain, he has tantrums, he needs to be wooed.'

However the late Beverley Baxter, a drama critic as well as an MP wrote a piece in 1949 complaining that, with the exception of Laurence Olivier and a few others, the English stage was in 'the grip of the bachelors'. He claimed that bachelordom, which in his more circumspect times was the euphemism he had to use for homosexuality, was 'against nature and therefore against art'.

Whatever the validity of Michael Billington's theory about the hermaphroditic element in great acting like Olivier's, and despite the 'girlishness' encountered by Kazan, there has always been decidedly more muscular Hermes than willowy Aphrodite in Olivier's performances (not only Margaret Leighton but any actress who has played opposite him will attest to the male sexuality he generates on stage). And in his private life there has never been any suggestion that he was in 'the grip of the bachelors'. From an early age he has been experiencing what Beverley Baxter called 'the blending harmonies of marriage and the occasional discords'.

His first marriage, to Jill Esmond, took place when he was twenty-two, appropriately at All Saints, Margaret St (where he had attended choir school and taken his first steps as an actor); and his third and last to Joan Plowright happened thirty years later at Wilton, Connecticut, USA. His second, and most celebrated marriage to Vivien Leigh in 1940, was also in the USA, in Santa Barbara, before a judge, who after pronouncing them man and wife, emitted an unexpected and unforgettable cry of 'Bingo'.

He once said, talking about the tragic death of his mother when he was only 13, that he had been 'looking for her ever since and I think I've found her in Joanie'. She is 22 years his junior, a considerable actress in her own right, and since the opening of the National a leading member of the same repertory company; but they have seldom appeared opposite one another in star parts, so they have avoided, whether by accident or design, the invidious and often bitchy comparisons of their talents which bedevilled his acting union with Vivien Leigh.

In an interview in the *Daily Telegraph Magazine* Joan Plowright recalled one night when Ingmar Bergman and her husband 'talked about both having ministers for fathers and what effect that had had on them. A certain amount of guilt complex. And maybe this compulsive need to work. An ingrained need to work. An ingrained sense of service.'

Olivier's guilt complex, which could probably be traced back beyond his father to his Huguenot Protestant ancestors is related no doubt to what he called in the same interview his 'self-detestation'.

'There were times when to be James Tyrone in *Long Day's Journey* was heaven compared with being me. If he hated himself the way I hate myself – then at least we had a partnership. It's a great relief to be in somebody else's shoes, dirtier though they may be and uncomfortable though they may be.'

Terence Rattigan can recall an occasion when Olivier was particularly guilt-ridden and self-critical. It was a house party at Notley Abbey and the guests were playing one of those crude games, which appeal to the mischievous childish streak that exists in most actors. The rules of the game have a black-and-white simplicity, and it is based on the proposition that people can be divided into two broad, four-letter, categories: they are either 'shits' or 'cunts' (with the exception of one world-famous star who has a category to himself as a 'shunt'). In the game's lexicon the former are defined as the self-seeking villains of the world (one of them would approximate to the 'bit of a bastard' Olivier referred to in his Tynan interview), and the latter are not exactly cast in the heroic mould but they are nice, well-intentioned, a bit ingenuous, and dangerously close to what W. C. Fields called 'suckers'.

All that happens during the game is that the name of a celebrity or friend, present or absent, is selected, and each player calls out instant categorization. When Olivier's name came up all the players, unhesitatingly and unequivocally, refused to cast him as one of the villains. He responded by loudly insisting that he had been misjudged. 'You've got me wrong. Completely wrong. I really *am* one. You'll see. You'll see. I'll prove it.'

At that time his guilt complex was being fuelled, as he confessed to friends, by the fact that his marriage to Vivien Leigh was breaking up, but his prophecy has never been fulfilled.

As some of his friends testify in this book he has at times shown a generosity of spirit, an altruism, a loyalty uncommon in a star of his magnitude. But what his wife calls his 'sense of service' extends far beyond the range of duties and obligations to friends and colleagues to his wider responsibilities as a leader of his profession; and it is linked to what Tony Richardson refers to as his intuitive sense of national moods and aspirations.

In a lesser man and artist this combination could add up to a degree of sanctimoniousness, but there was no trace of that when he said about his appointment as Director of the National Theatre in 1963 'I looked around as honestly as I could, and I hope without self-deception, and thought perhaps I was the fellow with the best sort of experience to start the thing going.'

No one can dispute the fact that Olivier from an early stage in his career acquired more experience in theatrical management and administration than any other leading actor. His first venture into management was in 1935 when he presented *Golden Arrow* with a newcomer who had been trained in Birmingham, called Greer Garson. It ran for only a fortnight and Olivier lost money, which he was fortunately able to recoup in the film studios, thus setting a 'swings and roundabouts' pattern for his later career which has greatly benefited the theatrical 'swings'.

There may be some form of poetic justice in the fact that with later films like *Spartacus* and *Bunny Lake is Missing*, Hollywood provided indirect and advance subsidy for Britain's National Theatre by paying our first player enough money to enable him to return to the comparative poverty of the stage, where he could enlarge his experience and develop his art in readiness for the call to Waterloo Road.

And there was unquestionably another dispensation of poetic justice in the fact that Olivier was invited to set up the National Theatre in Waterloo Road in what had been the home of the Old Vic, because in 1949 while touring in Australia he had been summarily dismissed as a director of the Old Vic. His co-directors Ralph Richardson and John Burrell, who had worked with him since 1944 and provided the Old Vic with a memorable period in its history, were also dismissed; the governors, while indulging in a pretence that the dismissals were voluntary retirements from office, let it be known that they were making changes in administration as a move toward the establishment of a National Theatre. The move, as it turned out, was retrogressive, and Olivier, as we now know, would have the last laugh. Obviously the backstage and boardroom politics behind the Governors' decision were complex, if not Machiavellian, and the full story has yet to be told; but there can be no doubt that Olivier, who reached one of the most impressive peaks of his career during that 1948-9 Old Vic season when he performed Lear and Oedipus as well as Richard III, was treated shabbily by an unappreciative board of governors.

The final twist of fate is that he has been obliged to announce his retirement as Director of the National before fulfilling his long-cherished ambition to move the theatre into its magnificent new home on London's South Bank. I am not suggesting that there are any parallels between the treatment received by Olivier from the Old Vic board in 1949 and from the National board in 1973, but it would be ingenuous to suppose that the backstage and boardroom politics at the National have been totally free of rancour and recriminations.

I do not propose here to explore the various rumours and conjectures which have circulated, and it is certainly too soon to sift the facts from the rumours. In the following pages John Osborne and William Gaskill, who speak from first-hand experience, give their highly subjective views about why a change in administration was necessary at the National.

There are of course other more objective views of what will become known as the Olivierean decade, some of which are given in this book; but it will be some time before it can be seen in the proper perspective and assessed accurately. The new regime with Peter Hall as director and Jonathan Miller, John Schlesinger and Harold Pinter as associate directors, will no doubt initiate changes in policy and direction, and it will of course encounter criticism too.

Meantime what next for Olivier as the National moves into its second phase with him as life president, and as he looks back on his first decade, probably in his self-critical way analysing his mistakes and misjudgements, but also, one hopes, savouring his triumphs and remembering that in his own words 'perhaps without me it wouldn't be there?'

He is not a rich man as he admitted in a recent television interview in America. By the flamboyant standards of show business he has never led a flagrantly extravagant life, and in fact he confesses to a 'mania for petty economy', following the genteel poverty of his boyhood when he was baptismally conditioned by having to follow his father into the bathroom and use the same water to keep the heating bills down. (He has referred to this so frequently and with such distaste it is clear that even with a father who was a High Anglican priest devoted to ritual, the water was not in any way holy or purifying.)

Apart from sizeable salaries for forays into films, which he has partly used to finance stage ventures, he has not earned the staggering amounts of money which can be picked up in other entertainment spheres and in city board rooms. Indeed our leading actor, after more than 50 years of toil and achievement, is a pauper compared with a pop star twanging his way through a few hit records, or a company director tanning his unacceptable capitalist's face in the Cayman Islands: so our society's scale of values remains indictable and Olivier will go on working. Two or three years ago he said 'I worry about my children and the future, dying and leaving nothing, and my wife with three hulking kids'. But of course even if he were inordinately rich he would give the same reply, as he did recently, when asked if he ever thought about retiring. 'No, never, never.'

When he was stricken by cancer and by thrombosis a few years ago he had to say to himself 'I may never act again': he then realized 'what acting meant to me after beefing about it all those years'. His theory, which may be unacceptable in strict medical terms but may have some psychosomatic truth, is that he got so angry that the malignancies took fright and disappeared.

He has admitted recently that he has been having difficulties about learning lines and suffering dangerous fits of nervousness, one of which on the opening night of *The Merchant of Venice*. forced him to take tranquillizers; but these are problems that can beset all actors of advancing years, and in his case they cannot have been lessened by the fact that he was also carrying the administrative burdens at the National.

He has said that he finds directing more satisfying and fulfilling than acting, but he has also said that if he hadn't been an actor he'd have 'gone mad'. Acting is the essential release for his volcanic energy, which is by no means spent, and which, hopefully, will fuel many more brilliant performances. Now of course age limits his range of choice, but he has tackled most of the big parts in the classical repertoire, or rather he has survived them, because as he once said, 'acting great parts devours you. They are cannibals. It is a dangerous game.' However it would be surprising if he decides he does not have enough acting muscle and sinew left for at least one of the great parts – perhaps even Lear, although that is the most devouring of them all.

Whatever happens his position as the first player, lord among actors, is unassailable. It was with his Richard III in 1944 that his claims to the position were first taken seriously by the critics and the public. Until then, though there had been talk of Olivier's sharpening rivalry, John Gielgud had been pre-eminent; and since then they have been compared endlessly, and often pointlessly.

The historic production of *Romeo and Juliet* in 1935 when they exchanged the roles of Romeo and Mercutio was the only time they have worked together. Olivier, attacking his first major Shakespearean role, set the style he was to follow in all the others. Spurning the traditional images of the character he set out, the bold iconoclast, to find what he hoped would be the truth, the reality behind the part. As he has often said he works, unlike the introverted Method actors, 'mostly from the outside in', starting with an exterior physical detail, a peripheral characteristic, and hoping it will lead to the truth at the core.

In an attempt to find an up-to-date truth he was led in 1937, after consulting the Freudian authority Professor Jones, to a Hamlet with a mother fixation, and in 1938 to an Iago who was homosexually in love with his Othello (a truth of which Ralph Richardson as Othello was blissfully unaware).

At the beginning Olivier stripped his Romeo of romantic embel-
lishments and presented him as a lusty Italian youth whose love
for Juliet was an earthy passion, not a spiritual devotion. He was
so choked with desire that he gulped the verse. He admitted later
that he thought Gielgud at that stage of his career was over-poetic.
In his book *Playback* Ronald Hayman quotes Olivier as saying,
'Gielgud seemed to me to be a little conscious of his gifts of music
and lyricism.' So Olivier purposely and rebelliously presented the
contrast, and the more prosaic he was, the more poetic Gielgud
became – 'I saw him (Gielgud) going a little further into the
expected field of florid elocutory renditions . . . almost singing it.'

In his search for reality over the years Olivier has not of course
turned a completely deaf ear to the poetry. Although James Agate
said about his 1937 Hamlet 'Mr Olivier does not speak verse badly.
He does not speak it at all', he has on occasions spoken it mag-
nificently, but he has perhaps been happier with declamatory
passages than with soft cadences; as he has said himself, 'I think
I'm associated more with trumpets than with strings'.

It may be that Olivier has more accurately echoed the deafening,
fortissimo age we live in than any of his contemporaries, but his
pre-eminence over his more muted rivals is not just a matter of
decibels: in a general sense he is the actor of his times. In style
and approach he is the direct acting descendant of Kean, about
whom Coleridge said that watching him act was like reading
Shakespeare by flashes of lightning: Olivier's flashes are laser
beams.

In his book *Letters from An Actor*, William Redfield writes
'Ironically enough Laurence Olivier is less gifted than Marlon
Brando. He is even less gifted than Richard Burton, Paul Schofield,
Ralph Richardson and John Gielgud. But he is still the definitive
actor of the twentieth century. Why? Because he wanted to be.
His achievements are due to dedication, scholarship, practice,
determination and courage. He is the bravest actor of our time.'

If by less gifted Mr Redfield means less dependent on what's
been called divine inspiration he may be right, but while others
have been waiting for the inspirational urge, Olivier's creative
energy, which I noted at the beginning of this introduction, as one
of his greatest gifts, has driven him on to brave something new.

It should be noted that his brand of bravery is very much of this
age. It is not piously directed at a search for the unattainable
sublime, the Holy Grail of tragic acting. Agate described him as

'a comedian by instinct and a tragedian by art', and he has been criticized for scaling down the Lears, the demigods and heroes of classic drama to his own dimensions as an actor; but in doing so he has brought them to the acceptance level of his irreverent, sceptical, twentieth-century audiences.

His wife has said, 'The theatre is his form of church', and, although his father's influence, as he has said himself, has left him with a taste for ritual and the Gothic, it is in parts a very modern church, straining a little perhaps to keep up with the times; if there is a stained glass window the colours are bold and sharp, and through it Archie Rice is looking with a slightly hesitant leer and a desperately hopeful wink.

LOGAN GOURLAY
London 1973

Dame Sybil Thorndike

LOGAN GOURLAY: How long have you known Laurence Olivier?

SYBIL THORNDIKE: Since he was nine years old. His father and my father were at side-by-side churches in Pimlico. Father Olivier was at St Saviour's and my father, Canon Thorndike, was at St James's. They were great friends, though Father Olivier was much the younger. They thought alike in church matters. One day Father Olivier said to my husband, Lewis, and myself: 'I wonder if you'd go and see my boy Laurence in a school play and tell me what you think of him.' It was at All Saints' in Margaret St. We knew the church and the vicar and off we went. The play was *Julius Caesar* and Larry was playing Brutus.

LG: How was he in the part at that age?

ST: He had been on the stage for only five minutes when we turned to each other and said: 'But this is an actor – absolutely an actor. Born to it.' You didn't have to tell him anything about Brutus; he seemed to know it all. His brother was playing Caesar. The difference was extraordinary. One was a boy giving a very intelligent performance and the other was a born actor. So we went home to his father Gerald and said: 'Your boy's born to the stage. You won't keep him off.'

LG: Did his father want to keep him off the stage?

ST: No, in fact he didn't. On the contrary, he was in favour. I think his father would have liked to be an actor himself. He was very dramatic in his sermons. And very sympathetic as a person. Elegant in appearance. Larry didn't look like him. He looked much more like his mother. She was rather gypsy-like and Larry had the same look as a boy.

LG: Did you see him in any other school plays?

ST: I saw him in *The Taming of the Shrew*, as Katharine. He was a wonderful Katharine – a bad-tempered little bitch. And he looked just like his mother in the part – gypsy-like. He must have been about ten or eleven at the time. I saw him in school plays till he was about thirteen. He played Sir Toby and Maria too, I think. He could play the girls beautifully. I remember years later when he was directing me in the film version of *The Prince and the Showgirl* he was showing me how to do something, and he said: 'You won't be able to do it as well as I could.' And it was true. He's marvellous in women's parts, though he himself is the least effeminate of men. You couldn't have a man less effeminate off stage. Yet I've seldom seen a better Katharine than the one he did at school. I remember they did it at Stratford. It was a remarkable production. They all were, those school productions.

LG: What made them so remarkable?

ST: Undoubtedly it was the director, Father Heald. He was a brilliant man with a great knowledge of the theatre. And he was a very fine priest, too. As a stage director he was way ahead of his time. His productions were more advanced than anything else in the theatre at that period. He was using the whole of the auditorium – using the aisle as well as the stage. He was very forward-looking and experimental.

LG: Do you think he had a strong lasting influence on the young Olivier?

ST: Definitely. I don't think he made Larry want to go on the stage. Nobody had to do that. As I've said, nobody could have kept him off. But I think Father Heald sowed the seeds in Larry that made him bold and adventurous in his work. Forward-looking. Never accepting the traditional for its own sake.

LG: Did you and your husband help him in his work when he left school?

ST: As a matter of fact we didn't see much of him just after he left school. He went on the stage professionally, as we knew he would, when he was about seventeen. He started with Barry Jackson at the Birmingham Rep. He came to us later, when he was still quite young, in *The Cenci*. Then I remember in *Henry* VIII he and Carol Reed held up my train. They were both in love with Angela Baddeley at the time – calf love – and they used to quarrel like mad. I used to say: 'You shut up, you two, and attend to what you're doing.'

LG: When he was attending to what he was doing was he impressive?

ST: Oh, yes. I remember in *The Cenci* he had to announce the Cenci to me. And he'd put on the face of the Cenci. More than the face. It was obvious that he was a highly sensitive actor. Yet he was never bucked with himself. Never too pleased with himself. He'd say: 'I don't think I can do this', when he was asked to try something new, and then he'd go ahead and do it.

LG: Did you think then that he was going to have an outstanding career and become a celebrated actor?

ST: No. We didn't think about it in those terms at that time. We just knew he was going to be a very fine actor. But we weren't career-minded then. People are much more so now. We didn't care whether we were in London or Timbuctoo as long as we were acting. There wasn't nearly so much emphasis on stardom and publicity.

LG: Did he make many appearances with you in the early years?

ST: Not many. I used to think he was in *St Joan* with me, but he tells me he wasn't. I thought he was one of those youngsters who took my shackles off. But it was another youngster, Bernard Miles, who started the Mermaid. However I saw Larry quite often on stage and I remember I was impressed by his voice and pitch. Whatever he did he was always there ' on the middle of the note'. All musicians, particularly piano players, will know what I mean. Larry didn't have any formal musical education but his family background was musical, and that must have helped. His voice has a wide range. He's got a lot of notes in his voice – overtones on his low notes which are very good.

LG : Did he have any bad faults as a young actor?

ST : Well there was a period of about two years at the Birmingham Rep. when I thought he was rather slack – too easygoing. He must have been in a slack mood – going through a growing-up process. Yet you always knew he was there when he was on the stage because of that indefinable thing – personality. That's what makes all the difference. Acting technique by itself isn't enough. I've always said that acting is a natural thing and any intelligent person can do it, if he can lose self-consciousness. But personality gives the extra dimension. And it's either there or it isn't. It cannot be learned. Now Larry has had it from the beginning. A distinctive personality. You can't help watching him when he appears even in a small part. Remember his Button Moulder in *Peer Gynt* with Ralph Richardson. Not a big part but Larry was extraordinary – unforgettable.

LG : You appeared with him in *Peer Gynt* didn't you?

ST : Yes. It was during the war when Larry and Ralph started the Old Vic again and they asked me to join them. It was the first time I'd appeared with him since the early days. It was wonderful. One of the plays we did was *Arms and The Man*, with Larry as Sergius. We opened in Manchester and Larry was frightfully funny I thought, but nobody laughed at him and he got no notices at all. He was furious and he couldn't understand it. The day after the opening he ran into Tony Guthrie in Deansgate. Tony said: 'You're looking rather gloomy', and Larry told him: 'It's that Sergius. I can't do him. I give him everything I've got but nobody laughs. I hate him.' Tony replied: 'If you hate him you can't play him. You must learn to love him.'

LG: Did he learn to love him?

ST: Yes, he had to. The point is you can't play any character unless you learn to love him and understand him. However beastly the character is you've got to find something to love in him. I know that very well from my own experience. I've had to play such cows sometimes, but I had to find something sympathetic in them – something I could sympathize with – before I could play them convincingly. After he learned that lesson Larry became very funny and convincing as Sergius.

LG: What was his most outstanding performance at that time?

ST: The *Oedipus* without doubt. That was memorable. Quite remarkable. It's an amazing play. Like a modern whodunit. Larry went for pure realism in the part. He didn't strive for anything more, but something in himself made it larger and bigger. He wanted to be down-to-earth rather than poetic, but his performance took on higher qualities. I think it's one of the best things he's ever done in tragedy.

LG: What do you think of his other tragic performances in the classics. His Lear for example?

ST: Let me say first of all that I think he's a much greater comedian than he is a tragedian. No one can match him as a comedian, but there are actors who can get farther than he has in tragedy – though they aren't really such good actors. A man like Johnny Gielgud, for example, has to work like blazes to get what he wants. He isn't such a natural actor as Larry, who is in fact the most natural actor I've ever come across. In a way it comes almost too easily for him. His Lear was frightfully interesting, but it wasn't one of the greatest Lears. This may sound paradoxical, but maybe it was because he's too good an actor. He didn't have to struggle enough. There must be struggle – a striving for something bigger than yourself in all forms of art – if you are to achieve greatness. And even then you don't always achieve it. It's something apart from what you are. Yet it's closely connected with what you are as a person – your attitude to life, your reaction to your own personal tragedies and troubles.

27

LG: What would you say is Olivier's attitude to life and how is it linked with his work?

ST: Whenever anything tragic has happened to him he's laughed at it and turned it to comedy. He'd laugh at fate before he'd go under. I don't mean that he's not capable of suffering – he is – but he's never dwelt on his own troubles and inflicted them on others. The tragedian is more self-centred, turned in on himself and his own agony – the agony of the world. Larry has never taken himself too seriously. He has very little conceit; none of that tortured egocentricity that some actors have. But without it perhaps you cannot be one of the greatest Lears or Othellos.

LG: What was your opinion of his Othello at the National?

ST: It was a fascinating study of a Negro – of a member of an oppressed race. But Othello wasn't a member of an oppressed race. He was a Moor, a proud man, bigger than any of the whites in the play. And apart from that I think Larry missed the deep agony in the part. I don't think he can ever do agony. Torture, yes, and personal torment he can do. Look at the *Oedipus* for example. But not the deep agony of an Othello. Now Ralph Richardson can get it. And he did years ago, incidentally, when Larry played a wonderful Iago to him. Michael Redgrave can get it too, and Johnny Gielgud. Their tragic performances can be greater than Larry's, because they've got something tragic in themselves. They're more deeply introspective than Larry is.

LG: How do you judge him in the other leading Shakespearean parts?

ST: I loved him as Hamlet, though I must admit I don't really know what is a great Hamlet and what isn't. I suppose I loved him partly because of its humour. Hamlets without a trace of humour are such bores. I think Larry was a very fine Macbeth when he played it years ago with Judith Anderson as Lady Macbeth. He may not have been one of the most memorable Macbeths, but then I think it's one of the most hellishly difficult parts for anyone to play. One of the reasons is that it's so difficult to get sympathy for him, and for her, without deviating at all from their wickedness. Then recently at the National I thought his Shylock was outstanding – terribly moving. He got the torment, the personal torture, especially at the end with the awful wail.

LG: What do you think has been his greatest part to date?

ST: The *Oedipus* perhaps. But I was forgetting his Richard. That was superb. His gifts as a comedian gave it that extra dimension and made you sympathize with Richard. As you should. But it's terribly difficult to select one part as the greatest. I can only talk about what has impressed me most – my own personal favourites.

LG: I'm told that his own favourite part – the one he feels most in sympathy with – is the Captain in Strindberg's *Dance of Death*. Have you heard that?

ST: No, but I can understand it, and I think he was excellent in the part. The suffering was there, the personal torment – if not the high tragedy – and the humour too. Grim humour, defiant humour; but he understands that, and he can play it brilliantly. His range is amazingly wide. I remember his double bill of Oedipus and Mr Puff. It was a *tour de force*. The critics were annoyed with him, I suppose, because they thought that technically he shouldn't have been able to do it. Critics are impossible. They complain about an actor trying to be too versatile and at the same time they complain even more if they think he has too narrow a range. Few of them have fully appreciated the breadth of Larry's range. I must confess I've been a bit critical at times because I've thought he's been too concerned about make-up. I used to think the same on occasions about my husband, Lewis [Casson]. Like Larry he loved to play around with false noses and wigs and beards. But of course it was just part of his craft. He was too good an actor to depend only on make-up. And so is Larry. An interesting thing about him is that when you see him off stage without make-up you'd never think he had such a mobile face. You can see in the films especially just how mobile and expressive it can be.

LG: What is your opinion of his Shakespearean films?

ST: Drivel in parts. No, that's not fair. I liked the Henry for one, but not as Shakespeare. As a spectacle – a pageant. Generally I don't think the screen is a good medium for Shakespeare, but then I must admit it's not a medium I really understand. I suppose I'm too old-fashioned for it. When I was in that film version of *The Prince and the Showgirl* with Larry and Marilyn Monroe I couldn't hear a word she was saying as I watched her doing her first scenes. I said to myself: ' Is this the great young star from Hollywood? I think she's awful.' I said as much to Larry and he said: ' Come and see the rushes, darling.' Well, I did, and everything she'd done that I'd thought was a muck-up came over beautifully on the screen. *I* was the old ham. I'm afraid I've never mastered the movie technique. It always looks underplayed to me – a bit careless.

LG: Has Olivier mastered it?

ST: He has a flair for acting in any medium. However, with his early stage training he had difficulties when he first appeared in front of the cameras. He told me that he thought he'd never get the hang of it at the beginning, but of course he did and he became a superb screen actor. I think his real love will always be the stage, though. He's more at home there. Now with Vivien – Vivien Leigh – I think it was the opposite. She preferred the screen, though she did some excellent things on the stage. She could be very impressive in the right stage part. When they were married they did some marvellous productions together in both mediums. She had wonderful qualities as an actress. But her beauty was against her. Great beauty like hers can be a damning thing – a handicap as much as an asset. I was very fond of her. Poor girl, she suffered hell. But so did Larry. God help us. I'm afraid I interfered a bit. I interfered, too, in his first marriage to Jill Esmond. Before his last marriage to Joan Plowright he said to me: ' Look here, you've interfered twice. Don't do it again. Stop it.'

LG: When you say you interfered, do you mean you gave him advice?

ST: Advice! I gave him hell. I was furious. I was brought up in the Church, as he was, and I hate divorce. Once you've given yourself to someone, well, if things go wrong you've just got to lump it. By today's standards I suppose that makes me an old fuddy-duddy, but that's what I believe.

LG: Among the modern parts Olivier has played is there one you would select as his best?

ST: Once again it's difficult to pick one out. Besides I'm afraid I haven't been able to see them all. I missed him in *The Entertainer*, for example, and I believe he was superb. One I particularly remember, though I've forgotten the title [*Semi-Detached*] – but it was the one in which he played an ordinary chap in Nottingham. It was an amazing performance, and how he got that beastly Nottingham accent so accurately I'll never know.

LG : It has been said that he is the only one of our leading actors who could have been so successful in the difficult job of founding and developing the National Theatre. What are the qualities that make him a good actor-manager, an administrator as well as an artist?

ST: It may sound flippant but I think he's been able to do such a good job at the National because he's a comedian. But a comedian in the best and fullest sense of that word. The tragedians are too self-centred for that kind of job. Larry has an enormous appreciation of other people's efforts. They can work with him and for him, because they know he's not just working for himself. His unselfishness makes him a good manager and director. It also makes him the lovable person he is off stage. I feel a bit maternal towards him – he is in fact just a little bit older than my eldest son. However that doesn't mean that I see him with a mother's rose-coloured glasses. I haven't agreed with him about a lot of things and I've told him so. Still, when I talk about any limitations he may have in the great tragedies I'm being hypercritical. Like all great artists Larry is aware of his own limitations – what he can do and what he cannot do. Yet he doesn't always know what he can achieve, because that's bigger than himself. He's bigger than he knows.

Max Adrian

LOGAN GOURLAY: When you first encountered Olivier in the 1920s were you immediately aware of his potential as an actor?

MAX ADRIAN: Yes, I had no doubt whatsoever that he would have a brilliant career. However at that time he must have thought himself that he had just made a serious mistake. He had turned down *Journey's End*, after appearing in its first one-night performance, in favour of *Beau Geste*, which was a terrible flop. Still it may be that his decision wasn't such a bad one. Although he appeared only briefly in *Journey's End* he was seen by the people who mattered and they saw him again, showing that he could play a different kind of part, in *Beau Geste*. Even in a bad part he could make some impression on an audience. And of course given the right material he was electrifying. He's always had that ability to make an audience instantly aware of his presence on a stage.

LG: Do you think he felt himself in the early stages of his career that he would become one of our leading actors?

MA: I think he had doubts and worries about some of his performances, as every actor has. But I don't think he had any real doubts about his final emergence as a leading actor.

Yet he needed reassurance frequently, and he still does, which is extraordinary because over the years he's had reams and reams of reassurance and praise from the world's press. Certainly he's had some bad notices from the press, but on the whole he's had many more good ones than bad ones. Deservedly, too.

LG : What do you think has been his greatest performance ?

MA : Without doubt his Richard III with the Old Vic at the New Theatre at about the end of the war. It was sheer genius. Next I think I'd place his Astrov in *Uncle Vanya* at Chichester and the National. In the modern plays there's one performance that stands out above all the others and that's Archie Rice in *The Entertainer*.

At the other end of the scale his Lear with the Old Vic at the New Theatre was a failure. I hated it and I told him so. Of course he doesn't like your hating any performance of his, though he should know himself that he cannot excel in every one.

Yet he can laugh at himself on occasions. I remember once we happened to be in Hollywood at the same time and we watched one of those old movies on late-night television. It was *Rebecca*, in which he played a glamorous young man. Watching it years later he made fun of himself in a way that no critic has ever done.

LG : You appeared with him in the film version of *Henry* v. Had you acted with him before ?

MA : No and I almost didn't appear in *Henry* v. When he was preparing for the film he asked me to do a test for the part of Fluellan. I thought he must have taken leave of his senses and I said so. I told him I thought I was totally unsuited for the part. But he was insistent, so I went to the studios one morning and they made me up with a beard. Then they put me in a suit of armour and stuck a heavy steel helmet on my head. Larry took one look at me and said, ' You'd better do the test sitting down.'

Well it was a disastrous test, as I'd feared it would be, and I'm afraid I laughed in the middle of it. He wasn't pleased at my laughter but he had to admit that I wasn't at all right for the part. Anyway he forgave me for proving him wrong and a little later he asked me to do another test, for the Dauphin. Just after I'd done it, while we were still on the studio floor, he said that he liked it very much indeed. However about a week later he wrote to say that he didn't like it so much when he saw it on the screen, and would like more time to make up his mind. That's show business and I was fairly certain he would cast someone else. He did, and off they went to Ireland to start shooting the film. But to my astonishment he rang me up about a week later from Ireland, saying he had changed his mind and asking me over to play the part.

 On the first day's shooting I told him I didn't feel at all confident because I was afraid I was second choice for the part. But he assured me he had wanted me from the beginning. Whether it was true or not, he was able to put me in the right frame of mind and give me the necessary confidence. He's very good at doing that because he knows exactly how an actor feels, and how he reacts in any given situation. Of course by the same token he knows exactly how to wound an actor when he wants to.

Anyway, everything worked out very well on the film and on the whole it was a happy and rewarding experience. I've always enjoyed working with Larry. He's stimulating and he can be inspiring. Something has always told me, however, never to ask him for a job, and I never have. I've always waited until he approached me.

LG: When did he approach you again after *Henry* v?

MA: Not until he was making plans for the National, though we had kept in touch over the years and we had become closer friends.

When he did ask me to join the National I remember he said: ' We need old character tats like you.' So I signed on and I was in practically everything in the first year, starting with *Hamlet* and following with *St Joan, Uncle Vanya* and *The Recruiting Officer*.

Although I was being worked so hard there was a bit of niggling about money, I remember. My agent insisted on a certain amount and Larry didn't agree at first. I suppose he had a tight budget and that first year's company was a fairly expensive one. Subsequently he's had less expensive companies, and I think he's also preferred to have actors whose contracts don't give them a veto on parts as mine did. But I found that the veto was very necessary. For example Larry wanted me to play a part in *Othello* that I would have been completely unsuited for. Fortunately I was able to exercise the veto and stay out of *Othello*. I didn't find anything about the production very appealing.

Over the years I'd heard Larry say that if he played Othello he would be careful not to let some Iago run away with the production. He had played it himself years before at the Old Vic with Ralph Richardson as Othello. Well, it seemed to me he was protecting himself at the National by casting Frank Finlay as Iago. Not that Frank is a bad actor. On the contrary he's a very good one, but he had played only one Shakespearean part before, and that was the gravedigger in *Hamlet*. He lacked the experience in Shakespeare for a part like Iago. And the temperament too. Frank is gentle and non-aggressive. He's not a typical actor as Larry is, and as I am. We're selfish bastards on occasions, but Frank is not. He's unassuming and he's easily crushed.

Larry gave me seats for the first night of *Othello* but I told him I wouldn't go because I didn't want to be present at the sacrifice – the showing-up – of Frank Finlay. I gave the seats away. I never saw the production, but I'm told that after a time, in a curious way, because of the part itself, Frank became more and more powerful in it. So the final irony if you like is that Shakespeare takes his revenge on actor-managers who try to dominate one of his plays completely.

LG: Do you know of any other occasions when Olivier has behaved like this?

MA: No, I don't. As far as I know he's never been guilty of doing that except in *Othello*. I think he wanted to prove something then – something he didn't have to prove – which was that he was the greatest actor in our midst. But there was no doubt about that, and all he succeeded in doing was proving that even the greatest can make great big mistakes.

However it should be remembered that from the beginning at the National he had been burdened by all kinds of problems.

The first year in particular was sheer hell. I remember when we got on to the stage at the Old Vic to rehearse the *Hamlet* the whole place was still littered with rubble and mortar, and there was a bloody enormous hole in one wall which allowed the wind to blow straight in from Waterloo Road. It was frightfully uncomfortable and chaotic. Then to add to the problems we had a very complicated, overpowering set by Sean Kenny. He's a delightful and talented Irishman, but I think he went too far on that occasion. I said to him after falling over bits of the set for the hundredth time: ' I suppose this is your revenge on the English.'

There were moments during rehearsals for that very first National production when I thought we'd never open. I kept thinking back to the time in Hollywood when Larry had told me in confidence that he had been asked to run the National and he had accepted. He was thrilled by the prospect – so were we all – but at the same time he had said: ' I'll be the most hated man in England.' I'd said: ' You'll certainly be the most powerful man in the English theatre, but you won't be hated unless you behave badly.'

He certainly hasn't behaved badly, but perhaps he has behaved stupidly or ill-advisedly at times because of the strain of being the administrator as well as the star performer. It's an impossible task for one man – even one with his enormous energy and talent.

LG: Despite the discomforts and problems, I don't suppose you have any regrets about being at the National during that first year?

MA: Of course it was fascinating to be in at the beginning of something as theatrically important as the National, but I do regret the fact that some of the problems and difficulties that could have been avoided weren't avoided. And I must say I wasn't happy during that first year. I don't think the rest of the company were either. And Larry must have been at least partly responsible.

I'm afraid all his success and acclaim have not made him a happy man. He used to be very different. Off stage no one could be more amusing, stimulating and interesting, particularly when he was talking about the theatre. He could be very disarming, too, discussing his own performances, and saying about one that had been highly praised that he himself had thought that it was bloody awful. As a *raconteur* he could be superb. He used to tell a story about a snake and a chicken in the zoo. Every day the snake used to be given a live chicken, which it immediately gobbled up. But one day a rather brave little chicken was put into the cage and it pecked fiercely at the snake, which was so surprised that it reared up and died of a heart attack. Not the greatest story perhaps, but as he told it Larry became the chicken and the snake, and he was so convincing that at the end, when he was playing the snake, you thought he was going to have a heart attack himself and pass out on the spot.

LG: Apart from the pressures of his job at the National do you think there is any particular reason for the fact that, as you say, he is not a happy man? Has he any regrets about the past? Any unfulfilled ambitions?

MA: I think he regrets the onrush of years, which seems to speed up as you get older. The years seem to fly away when you get into your sixties. But nothing can be done about it. We have to accept it philosophically. And Larry in particular must have a tremendous sense of achievement when he looks back. He's had more success on the stage than any other actor of his time. He's also the first working actor to become a member of the House of Lords. I used to call him Lord South Bank. A bit irreverent perhaps and I don't think he liked it very much, but it was meant affectionately. And it's certainly appropriate because he has given his all to creating that theatre on the South Bank. If he hasn't been a happy man recently it must have something to do with the fact that he has been carrying all the business worries as well as the artistic responsibilities.

I don't think he's particularly good at the business side. He's very generous, I know, in his personal relationships, and I think he tends to be too extravagant as a manager.

It's said that *Macbeth* is the unluckiest of Shakespeare's plays, but I think in Larry's case it must be *Hamlet*. Apart from anything else I don't think he understands the part particularly well. He's never excelled in it himself and when he came to direct Peter O'Toole in that opening National production I don't think he helped Peter very much.

LG: It has been said that Peter O'Toole's attitude during that production was unprofessional.

MA: He's high-spirited – what they used to call a hell-raiser. But thank God there was someone around like him to raise our spirits and break the tensions, even if he indulged in a few schoolboy's practical jokes like putting ice in the shower in the star dressing room, which Larry had lent to him.

Peter got it into his head that I couldn't get through a performance without a bottle of what he called 'green whiskey' – Irish whiskey. The truth is I loathe and detest the stuff, but he would try to pour it down my throat.

The star dressing room became a sort of oasis of relaxation while he was there, and I'm afraid it became a much duller and stuffier place when Larry took it over again.

Still, I mustn't give the impression that Larry is a stuffy, puritanical ascetic. He likes to live well. He enjoys good food and wine. And he's an excellent host. That reminds me of one occasion when we were both working in Hollywood, and I confess I was anything but a good host. I used to charge him $2 for his dinner. It's not as mercenary as it sounds, however. We happened to be living in the same apartment block on Sunset Boulevard and he wasn't in the best of spirits at that time. He hated the film he was working on – *Spartacus*, I think it was. His marriage to Vivien Leigh was breaking up, and he was lonely and needed company.

I like to cook and I was preparing a meal every night, but I thought if I invite him to dinner regularly he'll feel duty bound to sit around after dinner being polite. So I struck on the idea of asking him to pay $2 for each dinner. I used to present him with the bill every Saturday and he paid up. It turned out to be a very good idea because it freed him of any feeling of obligation, so he was able to relax and he often stayed on after dinner chatting and talking out his troubles. I wasn't casting myself as a father confessor but I think I did him some good by just being a good listener. Anyway, I felt closer to him as a human being at that time than I have before or since, and I think he appreciated the fact that I was at least lending a sympathetic ear.

Nowadays I think he regards me at times as a tiresome old chap. However I think he can be quite tiresome himself in some ways. But that doesn't affect my friendship for him. I've got great affection for him, and I think he's a much better man than I am – a much better specimen of humanity. He's got a great sense of responsibility, which I lack. He's been very helpful in a quiet way to friends who've been in trouble. He's been surrounded by people who've been dependent on him financially to varying degrees. Still that's rather in the tradition of the great actor-managers, isn't it?

He's a strange mixture of contradictions. He can be magnanimous at one moment, impatient and ready to take offence the next. I remember one night at a party I gave in Hollywood a young actor said something to him about the have-nots in the profession. I think he was suggesting that the stars might do more to help them. Larry flared up immediately. He was like a fighting cock and he told the unfortunate young actor in no uncertain way that the stars couldn't be responsible for people who probably shouldn't have come into the profession in the first place. Larry was probably right, but he overreacted and got it out of proportion.

Of course he's a great realist about what they call the relationship of the actor to society. He always points out that the world doesn't owe us a living. If we want respect and rewards from the public we've got to work and earn them. Larry himself had to struggle for everything at the beginning of his career. His father was a clergyman who couldn't subsidize him or open any doors for him. Still, he had given Larry the right background and upbringing. I think some of the best parts of Larry's character come from the early religious influences.

LG: Has religion remained a strong influence on his life?

MA: I think it has, up to a point. He still has a great interest in religion, and I know he has found great solace in religion when he has been troubled emotionally. I myself try to live as a Christian should, and he's often said to me: ' Say a prayer for me when you go to church.' And he meant it. He wasn't saying it in a glib, facetious way.

I think on occasions he himself has probably said a few silent prayers for his friends. He can be very sympathetic and considerate. He can understand people's faults and weaknesses – though he can't always forgive them. I'm sure he knows his own faults too – some of them anyway. But I'm not sure if he forgives himself.

Sir Noël Coward

I believe Laurence Olivier to be the greatest actor of our time. Although I have no intention of qualifying this statement I am prepared to explain, briefly, my reasons for making it.

During the 1930s I directed him in three plays: *Private Lives*, *Theatre Royal* (the English production of Edna Ferber's and George Kaufman's *The Royal Family*) and *Biography* by S. N. Behrman. In those, his young days, he was trying his wings, and never once did he flap them vulgarly. To me, vulgarity in the theatre does not necessarily mean four-letter words or slapstick – it means overacting, striving for illegitimate laughs and not playing true.

I have seen Larry being outrageous in the theatre. His performance, for instance, of Sergius in *Arms and the Man* was a most hilarious and almost disgraceful bit of play-stealing, but curiously enough it somehow was not overacting. It stayed within his own (admittedly widely stretched) conception of the part. His Mr Puff in *The Critic* and his Captain Brazen in *The Recruiting Officer* were both pure masterpieces of farcical playing. As Malvolio his assumption of pompous, seedy grandeur, his agonizingly refined cockney accent and his ultimate pathos will never leave my memory.

Now I should like to mention two of the parts he has played that were neither specifically comic nor tragic, but quiet, psychological studies that lie between those two extremes: Astrov in *Uncle Vanya* and Solness in *The Master Builder*. In both these divergent roles his authority, repose, subtlety and impeccable truth of characterization were beyond praise.

His greatness as a tragedian has been an accepted fact now for many years. His Richard III, Henry V, Macbeth and Coriolanus, to name only four, were all endowed with imagination, strength, originality and dazzling theatrical flair. His latest great classic role is Othello and it is, to my mind, one of his finest achievements yet. In the first place Othello is one of the most difficult parts ever written. It is a series of exhausting climaxes based on what has always seemed to me to be a fairly silly premise. Larry's conception of it has aroused a certain amount of controversy, the principal argument against it being that it is too Negroid. In my opinion, which perhaps need not be taken too seriously as I am far from being a Shakespearean expert, it is this that stamps it with originality. I have seen too many 'Noble Moors' musically declaiming their anguished jealousy, and I have seldom been moved by any of them. In any case I am so subjugated by Larry's dedicated talent that I would fly to see him if he elected to play Hamlet as a Chinaman.

In addition to his initial genius for acting, his imagination and the meticulous concentration with which he approaches every part he plays, he has always had and still has the physical attributes of a romantic star. True, in his earlier, halcyon days at the Old Vic he made every effort to disguise these with acres and acres of nose paste and false hair. I cannot think of any other living actor who has used such quantities of spirit-gum with such gleeful abandon. I believe that this rather excessive determination to be old before his time was the result of an integral shyness in his character. He has never had the smallest inclination to look or be himself on the stage. He is now the head of our English National Theatre, possibly, I suspect, at considerable financial inconvenience to himself, but definitely to the pride and honour of the profession to which he has contributed so much.

Alan Webb

I have known Laurence Olivier for the best part of fifty years.

In the early 1920s he was a young man whose dark hair grew low on his forehead and whose front teeth were broken as the result of a blow from a hockey ball or stick during his schooldays. In those far-off days, for a 'juvenile' to get his chance on the London stage it was almost imperative that he should be tall, with golden hair and blue eyes. I remember thinking that Larry would have to have exceptional talents if he were to get his oar in, so to speak.

At the time we were both working with a stock company in a production of *Julius Caesar*. Looking back it must have been a fairly ludicrous affair, and this evidently struck Larry forcibly because at one rather important point in the play he was overcome by ill-concealed laughter. On the top of a bus going home after the show I remonstrated with him, and told him he would surely never succeed unless he took his work much more seriously. At the same time I was secretly impressed by what seemed to me to be his fearlessness and by what I can describe only as youthful panache.

My recollection is that he got into very hot water with our management.

Only a few months after this he embarked on what was to be a great career in the theatre. He was fortunate, although at the time it must have seemed otherwise to him, that the productions he appeared in early in his career did not enjoy long runs and he was able to play a variety of parts.

I believe his first essays in management were not very successful. Indeed I remember people suggesting that he would never appeal to a large public, as his personality was not

simpatico. I suspect that the kind of play that was then supposed to appeal to West End audiences did not allow him to
show his great qualities.

Many years later I had a part in a celebrated production of
Titus Andronicus with Larry in the name part. My part was
small, but it involved a good deal of standing alone on the
stage with Larry and occasionally speaking a line or two while
he went through a storm of emotions. At one point he was
kneeling half back to the audience and preparing to chop off
his hand with an axe. I was transfixed, and I wondered what
must be passing through his mind. I think it must have been
during the first performance when, to my horror, just as the
axe was about to fall, out of the corner of his mouth he said
sharply: 'Get out of my light!' I was most upset and extremely
mortified, and as consolation I said to myself: 'He cannot be
really in his part if he's thinking about the lights.' I realized
later that it was the highest kind of professional behaviour.

In the same production, feeling somewhat frustrated, I said
to him: 'It's all very well for you. You have only to stand in
the middle of the stage and let it all pour out of you.' Larry
was amused and I am sure he did not believe that I thought I
could do what he was doing if given the chance. Indeed I was,
perhaps half-consciously, paying him a high compliment. The
more beautifully any action is executed the easier it tends to
appear to the looker-on. As with all great artists, his work
appears effortless, though surely he takes the greatest pains.
Small examples occur to me. I shall never forget my amaze-
ment when during a farewell speech from the stage at the end
of a season at Stratford-upon-Avon he mentioned by name the
entire theatre staff back and front of the house – a very considerable number indeed. And again on a continental tour in
front of and behind the Iron Curtain he addressed the various
audiences in their native tongues. One always likes to compare
the leading actors of one's own time with what one knows
and imagines of the great actors of the past. I like to think of
Laurence Olivier as the David Garrick of my time.

Emlyn Williams

LOGAN GOURLAY : Olivier and you are about the same age and you've both had long and distinguished careers in the theatre, but you've never worked together. Is there any reason?

EMLYN WILLIAMS : No. Just luck. Bad luck from my point of view, but I'm not sure if he would agree. Certainly we've both been in the theatre for a long time though he's had a much more distinguished career as an actor than I have, but a very important point is that we're not the same age. I am three years older.

I remember when we met on one occasion he said : 'You're still three years older than I am, aren't you?' I replied : 'Yes of course.' And he said : 'Stay that way for God's sake. Stay that way.'

LG : How old were you then?

EW : I honestly can't remember. Bad memory for dates. Anyway he was at the height of his career. For that matter he's always seemed to be at the height of his career. Anyway whenever we met after that he'd always say, 'You're still three years older aren't you?' Or we'd have a variation like 'I'm always specially delighted to see you because you're still three years older and still going strong.' It became the kind of running joke with variations that actors have who share the same dressing-room.

LG : You said he's always seemed to be at the height of his career. Is there any period when you think he's been at the very pinnacle?

EW : It's difficult to say; he's had so many high spots. What

46

is remarkable is the way he has sustained his success and achievement from one decade to the next. At the same time of course he's had his set-backs and failures particularly in the early years.

A long time ago when I was doing *Night Must Fall* and at the same time filming *Broken Blossoms*, he came to the studios one day with Glen Byam Shaw, who was a very close friend. Glen, I remember, took me aside and said 'Please be specially nice to Larry. He's terribly depressed – almost suicidal – about the notices he's had for *Romeo*.'

LG: That would be the Romeo he did with John Gielgud in 1935 when they exchanged the parts of Romeo and Mercutio.

EW: Yes, Larry opened first as Romeo and was massacred by the critics. He's never been very lucky with that play. A few years later when he did it with Vivien on Broadway, they had a terrible flop. In fact the New York notices were so bad Larry decided to offer the public their money back. And they took it. Long after, he and Vivien used to tell the story about sitting in the box-office giving the money back, and they were very funny about it, but at the time it must have been sheer hell.

LG: Do you think there's something about the part of Romeo or the play that makes it unsuitable for his talents?

EW: No, not at all. In each case the bad notices were due to a combination of other factors. On Broadway one of the factors I think was that the New York critics were prejudiced in advance about Larry and Vivien whom they regarded at that time as Hollywood movie stars who had no right to be tackling Shakespeare. In the earlier production with John Gielgud he had been trying a more realistic, or naturalistic, interpretation of the part, and at that time the critics weren't ready for it. Funnily enough Larry was more suited to both parts – Romeo and Mercutio – than John Gielgud was. John must have realized this in a way, yet he had invited Larry to join him in the production. It was very generous of John because at that time he was regarded as our leading classical actor and his reputation was much greater than Larry's.

LG: Would you say it's the other way round nowadays?

EW: I like to say that they share the top acting honours. I wouldn't like to say that one is greater than the other. They're both great in their distinctive ways. What's so fascinating is that their acting is so different in style, technique and texture. John might appear to be more limited because he's always himself. But that in a way is more difficult to do than to play Oedipus and Mr Puff in one evening. John could play Oedipus but I wouldn't like to see him as Mr Puff. And I'm sure he wouldn't like to see himself. But that doesn't mean that he's a lesser actor.

Indeed you could argue that because Larry is different in every performance he's just a rep. actor, who should confine himself to a rep. company. Then if you're arguing from the other point of view you could say that the very fact that Larry is different in every performance makes him a greater actor with a wider range. At that stage of course you start saying: ' Ah, it depends what you mean by great acting. What is your definition and so on . . .' All I can say is, thank God we've got them both with their different approaches and talents.

LG: Many of the people I've talked to about Olivier select his *Richard* III at the New with the Old Vic as the greatest of his differing performances. Would you agree?

EW: Yes I think so. I was specially interested and impressed because I'd played the part myself with the Old Vic in 1937 – about seven years I think before he did it. So I knew how difficult it was. My performance I'm afraid wasn't in the same league as his. He did things with the part that were astonishingly subtle. He made Richard sardonic, cruel and warped, but he also made him amusing – even sympathetic at times. He made him a very real person which is extremely hard to do. I was filled with admiration, spiced with envy.

LG: Did he see you when you played the part?

EW: Yes, he came to a matinée and came round to my dressing room afterwards. I can't remember what he said about the performance, but I do remember a small personal detail. He said: 'Vivien sends her regards. She's outside in the car. She's sorry she can't come round but she knows you'll understand.' At that time they weren't divorced from their first partners and in those days the attitude to marriage and infidelity was less permissive than it is now; so it was all a bit difficult for them and they were forced to be a bit clandestine. But they behaved very well in the circumstances. Just as they did many years later when their marriage was breaking up. As far as possible they discouraged their friends who knew, and loved them both, from forming into rival camps. So there wasn't as much bitterness as there might have been.

LG: What did you think of their performances together? At one time it was suggested by some newspapers – particularly when they did the two Cleopatras – Shaw's *Caesar and Cleopatra* and Shakespeare's *Antony and Cleopatra* – that he deliberately played down to give her an opportunity to shine.

EW: Nonsense. That was snide press misinterpretation. If the two Cleopatras weren't completely successful there were other reasons. His dedication to his job, his conscientiousness as an actor, his professionalism would never allow him not to give of his best. Certainly he was devoted to Vivien, but he was also devoted to his craft. In other words he could never be faithful to one love by being unfaithful to another.

I remember some people were always trying to make comparisons between her acting talents and his. Odious comparisons and rather silly. Certainly he had more experience in the classics than she had. But she was a considerable actress in her own right. Sensitive and highly intelligent.

LG: If you had to sum him up in a phrase or two what would you say?

EW: That I couldn't. If I had worked with him it might be easier. Or it might be more difficult. I don't know. All I can say is that off stage I've always found him a delightful and amusing companion. Never pompous and grand.

I have a house in Corfu and he spent a holiday there a few

years ago – very much a family holiday. He was with Joan and their two young children. I think they've been marvellous for him – given him a new lease of life. It was difficult to believe when you saw him sitting on the beach in his bathing shorts and playing with the kids that here was the famous, and the great, Olivier. He looked, and behaved, more like a barrister or a bank manager. In fact I've never seen him behave like the great actor off stage. But there's no doubt about what he is when he steps on to the stage. He's the complete professional.

I remember when he was doing that brilliant Richard III that everyone remembers I met him at a party and he asked me about a bit of business I'd used when I had been playing the part years before. He said he'd like to borrow it, but wanted my permission first. At first I couldn't remember much except that it was something I'd done with the Bible, but he reminded me. When Richard was trying to look pious in front of the crowd I'd made him read the Bible but then show himself up by turning the pages too quickly for reading.

I was enormously flattered a) that he should remember my performance in any detail and b) that he should want to borrow from it when his own performance had been hailed as matchless and unsurpassed. It's interesting that he wouldn't borrow without asking my permission first, and of course ironical that I'd forgotten what he wanted to borrow. It's a very good example of his sheer professionalism.

LG: Which do you think have been the most outstanding of his more recent performances at the National?

EW: I was enormously impressed by *The Master Builder*. But I must declare my interest. I wrote the adaptation. I did it originally for Michael Redgrave who meant to present it independently. Then when he joined the National it was one of the productions he said he would like to do. Larry took over the part from him and once again it would be a mistake to make comparisons. Let me just say that each was great in his own distinctive way.

The other performance by Larry at the National that I

will always remember, and u

LG: Were you worried, as ma
played it as a Negro?

EW: Not at all. I know some people .
a Negro was just a gimmick. But the rea.
to play Othello as a white man. I remember
ing Iago at Stratford to Harry Andrews as
asked: 'How are you doing?' and I said 'We
fairly straight, but I suppose the day will come wh
have a black Iago and a white Othello!' It's probab. .cn
done already in Czechoslovakia or somewhere. The point is
there has to be a colour question in the play. The question is
would you let your daughter marry Othello? At the same time
it would be wrong to have an Othello who was too obtrusively
coloured. But Larry's wasn't that. It wasn't Uncle Tom. It
was a marvellously subtle, intelligent and powerful performance. I hope he will go on to give many more as subtle, intelligent, and powerful. And I hope I will be around to see them.

LG: And to reassure him that you're still three years older.

Sir John Gielgud

LOGAN GOURLAY: What did you think of Olivier as an actor when you appeared with him in the 1935 production of *Romeo and Juliet*, alternating the parts of Romeo and Mercutio?

JOHN GIELGUD: He gave up a project to do *Romeo and Juliet* himself (with Jill Esmond to whom he was then married), and behaved towards me with great generosity and comradeship. His Mercutio was brilliant; his Romeo strikingly Italianate and romantic, though his verse-speaking was not then developed to the skilful level he has since accomplished.

LG: It has been said that Olivier is the greatest comic actor of the age. Do you share that view?

JG: I don't like these comparisons and distinctions. But let me say I will always cherish his Puff, Shallow and his Captain in *The Recruiting Officer* among his great performances in comedy. And in tragedy he was superb in *Titus*, *Macbeth* and *Richard* III.

LG: What are his outstanding qualities as an actor? And as a director?

JG: Attention to detail; complete assurance in his conception of character; athleticism; power; and originality.

LG: What do you think has been his greatest performance in Shakespearean plays?

JG: Macbeth, in my opinion, though it's difficult to choose from so many great performances.

LG: And in plays by other dramatists?

JG: The Captain in Strindberg's *Dance of Death*.

LG: Why do you think he has never become, as he has said himself, a big box-office screen star?

JG: At the time of *Wuthering Heights*, *Rebecca* and *Henry* V he was a romantic and successful screen star. Since that time he has changed to character parts and the vehicles he has chosen, *The Entertainer*, and an unlucky film with Jennifer Jones, were not commercially popular, though he has had many successes in less leading roles on the screen. His screen *Hamlet* and *Richard* III are still very popular in art theatres, and it is a great pity he was denied the backing for his screen version of *Macbeth*, which should have been sensational.

LG: What are the special qualities that have enabled him to run the National Theatre as well as play demanding principal parts?

JG: Dedication; industry; and a devotion to the task of being a leader of the theatre – even at the expense of his health, and opportunities to act himself.

Sir John Gielgud and Sir Ralph Richardson interviewed by David Frost*

DAVID FROST: You said once, talking of romantic success, that you loved playing somebody in love.

JOHN GIELGUD: Yes, but I couldn't do it. I tried very hard, but I don't think I was ever convincing as a lover. Laurence Olivier took over from me . . . we alternated Romeo and Mercutio in a very famous production in the 1930s, and I persuaded him to play both parts alternating every six weeks . . . when he played Romeo, I remember Ralph coming to see it and saying, 'He just stands against the balcony with such an extraordinary pose that this animal magnetism and vitality and passion come right over.'

I was very busy enunciating all the poetry very beautifully but I was very cold aesthetically compared to him. And I was struck then, as we all have been ever since, by his extraordinary power and originality, and the way he dashes with a part, and really wrings its neck without self-consciousness or worrying whether he's attractive or good or bad, or what. He's a great performer without caring, you feel, what is said. He doesn't act with the sort of caution and fear that some of the rest of us have.

I can't imagine what he would have done if he'd been rehearsing this play [Home]. I haven't worked with him as much as Ralph has. I've never really acted with him, except for that time so many years ago, and I'm always sorry I haven't. But I

*Excerpt from the David Frost Show on television in New York (11 Dec. 1970).

54

think he approaches a part with enormous confidence, dash and bravura. And Ralph and I are more cautious and we are more afraid of making mistakes – of throwing ourselves at a part as if it were a cage, and we could shake the bars off.

RALPH RICHARDSON: Yes, he's very bold. He's very, very bold.

Sir Alec Guinness

LOGAN GOURLAY: What did you think of Olivier as an actor when you first appeared with him in *Romeo and Juliet* in 1935?

AG: It was John Gielgud's production of *Romeo and Juliet* at the New Theatre. I was only the Apothecary and twenty-one years old, so not much of a judge; but I remember feeling jealous of Gielgud who, at that time, had no romantic rival in the English theatre. Larry Olivier was undoubtedly glamorous, but he seemed a bit cheap – striving after theatrical effects and so on – and making nonsense of the verse. Yet his personal success was undoubted, and he made himself look remarkably beautiful as Romeo. A year later I understudied him as Hamlet at the Old Vic and was outraged at the gymnastic leaps and falls required by his example. I never liked the performance or Guthrie's production, but it was a huge box-office success. Looking back at it with wiser hindsight I realize it was necessary for Olivier to do what he did – and it laid the foundations for his becoming a truly great actor.

LG: In the same season you played Sir Andrew Aguecheek to his Sir Toby Belch in *Twelfth Night*. Did it develop, as was reported at the time, into a nightly battle between you for the most laughs?

AG: Nonsense. Larry was always in charge of the stage and helped me enormously. Indeed he instructed me how to get laughs and, almost more important, when it was foolish to seek them. However, the production was not a success and I fear we all fooled about a lot – very unprofessional.

LG: It has been said that Olivier is the greatest comic actor of the age. Do you agree?

AG: I don't like 'the greatest' anything; it's always a rash judgement in my opinion. But Olivier has made me laugh more as an actor (in eccentric comic parts) than anyone else. In any case I love him in comedy and am *not always* sure about him in tragedy.

LG: What did you think of his 1946 *Lear*, in which you played the Fool?

AG: I hope he will play Lear again. I suspect that all first Lears are sketches for subsequent ones. I thought his 1946 *Lear* was wonderful in the storm scenes; he was actively moving every night in the lines that begin 'Poor naked wretches, whereso'er you are . . .', but I can't remember a great deal else about it, except benefiting myself from the lighting that always surrounded him as he kept the Fool close to his side.

LG: What do you think has been his best performance in Shakespeare and the classics?

AG: I can't believe the world will ever see a finer Henry V – a part for which he had every quality. And his Oedipus was superb as well. I wouldn't part with the memory of either of them, but neither would I part with his Mr Puff in *The Critic*. Alas, I never saw his Macbeth or Othello.

LG: What is your opinion of him as a screen actor?

AG: I don't see there is much difference in acting for stage or screen, but I feel that Larry needs a packed and attentive audience to enable him really to soar. Filming doesn't allow for that.

LG: What are the special qualities that have helped him to run the National Theatre so successfully?

AG: Sheer guts and determination, and total dedication to theatre.

LG: You have been his friend and colleague for thirty-five

years. Would you single out one particular virtue he has as a friend and as a man?

AG: A very warm sympathy to any actor in distress.

LG: If you were asked to choose an epitaph for him what would it be?

AG: There is a line under Reynolds's picture of Garrick (which depicts Garrick being torn in two directions by the allegorical figures of Comedy and Tragedy) that runs something like: 'Strive not, Comedy and Tragedy, to engage a Garrick who to all your parts does equal justice.' Something like that.

Sir Tyrone Guthrie*

Laurence Olivier is the son of a clergyman. In his youth he was a choirboy and went to a choir school. This means that two dominant influences on his formative years were music and liturgy. His theatrical career began when he was still very young at the Birmingham Repertory Theatre. His talent was immediately apparent. Before he was thirty he had played leading parts in London and New York; in a famous production of *Romeo and Juliet* he and John Gielgud alternated in the parts of Romeo and Mercutio.

This was the first time I saw him act. He had been severely faulted by the drama critics for what they regarded as bad verse-speaking. I thought he spoke the verse with marvellous clarity, energy and variety. What more can you want? He had, it is true, a tendency to rant; to make rather exaggerated contrasts of pace, pitch and volume. But these were the excesses of ardent, youthful temperament. Time would cure them. And, anyway, how rare it is to hear someone who can really blow up a storm, whose voice explodes like a bomb, crashes like breaking glass, screams like a macaw. A lot of the noises he made, and still makes, were not ' beautiful '; and drama critics, then as now, like their Shakespeare to be sonorous. In the interests of sonority they seem prepared to sacrifice most other values. I will confess that to me the Voice Beautiful is all too often the Voice Dull.

Laurence Olivier is never dull. The voice, however, has more the quality of brass than that of strings. And even now, after many years of intense cultivation and ceaseless practice, it is the vigour and brilliance of his tone that impress. Sweetness

*Excerpt from *In Various Directions* by Tyrone Guthrie, Michael Joseph, 1965.

does not come so easily. I have never been able to understand those critics who are not aware of the immense musicality that infuses all his performances – a rare sensitivity to rhythm, colour, phrasing, pace and pitch.

He has never been a particularly handsome man, but he has always been able, on the stage, to suggest extreme good looks. This is due partly to skill in make-up, but far more to the vitality and intelligence that inform every glance, and the athletic energy and grace of every movement.

He could have had – indeed briefly had – a dazzling career as a moviestar. But he has preferred to use the extraordinary opportunities that his gifts have presented to extend his expressive range rather than his fortune or fan-mail. Among his impressive achievements have been his screen versions of Shakespeare's *Henry v*, *Hamlet* and *Richard iii*. In my opinion, none of these was artistically successful. *Henry v* had some splendid moments of action but they had almost no relevance to Shakespeare's text and only helped to emphasize the chasm that separates stage play from screenplay. The achievement was to get these productions on to the screens of the world in the teeth of the timid and mercenary moguls of the film industry. But even Olivier's reputation, skill and formidable determination has not been able to realize his projected screen version of *Macbeth*. Eventually, perhaps, he will make it. But I hope that he will not allow his gifts to be squandered on what must in the nature of things only be a popularization, a reduction of a masterpiece.

One of the dangers of our times is that with enormously widespread and virtually instantaneous communication of ideas, success becomes overwhelming. There is no longer any possibility for an actor, an author or a musician to be modestly and reasonably successful. He is either practically unknown or else he is a household word from the North Pole to the South, from China to Peru. Successful artists cannot but be distracted by their success. They are too rich, confronted with too many attractive but confusing choices. If you are the object of a great deal of public attention it is difficult not to become self-important and not (even worse) to become nervous, over-anxious to please, afraid to offend.

In thirty years of celebrity Olivier has learned to handle the tricky business graciously and cleverly. But energy has had to be spent on this. I admire his art so wholeheartedly, love him so warmly as a friend and colleague that I grudge the time and energy that have to be spent on administrative work for the British National Theatre. Rightfully he is at its head. He was the right figurehead for its inception. He is doing a fine job. But it is not the job he does best. Much of what he is at present doing could be done equally well by several other people, none of whom could play Othello, Macbeth, Lear, Faustus and a dozen other great parts which, at present, he has no time to think about.

The years are passing. I suppose it is idle to wish it, but I'd like him to be less celebrated, less distinguished, less important and more free.

I want to see him abdicate. I want to see a sign that advertises: 'Throne vacant – Will suit hard-working, honest, methodical monarch.'

Angus McBean

I'm told that photographers are given a different view of people than are other, more ordinary mortals: 'How did you get on with so and so?' a friend asked. 'She was charming,' I said. 'You were lucky,' he answered, 'not a description I would use for that tiresome lady, but of course no one can afford to be unpleasant to one's photographer.'

Laurence Olivier and I started about the same time. He is four years younger than I am, but as I came to photography a bit late in my working life, I was not ready to photograph his earliest London appearances. But once I had started auspiciously with his first Hamlet at the Old Vic in 1936 I went on to photograph practically everything he did right up to the pictures I made for the film of *The Dance of Death* recently excepting only, alas, two wartime seasons at the Vic.

My sixtieth and Shakespeare's four-hundredth birthday happened to fall in the same year, and to mark this highly important occasion Messrs Kodak put on an exhibition of all the best of my Shakespeare photographs. Larry, in spite of being in the middle of that very taxing production of *Othello*, came and opened it for me.

Kodak had chosen the pictures themselves, so when Larry arrived and asked if we should walk round the exhibition, as I hadn't had time for a proper look I went with him. As we strolled he became a little restive, and when we came to a great board of Ivor Novello's *Henry* v he said: 'Not many of me, Angus, where's my *Henry* v?'

I was rather miserably explaining that I hadn't actually chosen the pictures myself, when we rounded a corner and there was a whole wall of Larry, including a ten-foot-high huge head of the current Othello, and all was well.

Larry then declared the bazaar open, made a long, amusing speech, presenting me in the end with a cake in the form of a camera nestling on a bed of sixty flash bulbs: very pretty and, as I found later, quite inedible.

Larry started by saying that ours was a happy and fruitful marriage of some thirty years' duration, howbeit photographic, then he went on to tell of our meeting. I was just at this time pushing at the doors of the theatre. I didn't know what I really wanted to do once inside, but it represented Art to me. I have always been good with my hands and I saw myself as a sort of freelance prop maker: a kind of poor company's Oliver Messel, and I had already had some small success as a maker of masks, very fashionable at that time. In my efforts to find more jobs I had met three girls who had also just started and who were working for the theatre under the name of 'Motley'. I had even done a few jobs for them, notably building most of the scenery for John Gielgud's production of *Richard of Bordeaux* and even fabricating all the shoes – 'Oh yes, I can make medieval shoes,' I heard myself saying, never having made a shoe in my life!

But that job was over and I had little work and less money. It was a beastly afternoon so I thought I would drop in on the Motleys; they at least would be good for a cup of tea.

They were then working in a building, said to have been Chippendale's workshop, in Mason's Yard opposite the New Theatre. It was much too romantic to last and has long since been swept away in the name of progress – I loved it.

The Motleys, I found, were away, and tea, alas, was clearly over. However there were two young men there. One was George Devine, Motley's new secretary and general factotum – new from Oxford. I had met him before, though we never really got on very well. He waved his hand towards the other, who was sitting in the dusk by the gas fire.

'Have you met?' said George.

The young man's face was covered with a mask of paint, and I looked quickly away. I am always bad at introductions.

So bad at making them that I can't accept them either; I find
I never listen or even look.

'Have you seen our play yet?' said George.

Romeo and Juliet had just been put on across the road and
the Motleys had done the décor. I had had nothing to do with
it. After all they now had George.

I hadn't been asked to sit down and I was just standing there
awkwardly. 'Oh no,' I said, 'I shan't go to it yet, I shall wait
for Olivier to come out and Gielgud to go in.'

It had been arranged, as quite a lot of other people in this
book will undoubtedly have told you, that John Gielgud, the
new young luminary of the period, should open as Mercutio,
while the even newer Laurence Olivier would carry Romeo; this
arrangement was to last for six weeks, when the positions
would be switched.

But we are still in the Motleys' studio in the winter dusk. It
was white painted, the only ornament being a delicate model
of a sailing ship in a clumsily contrived mirrored niche sunk
into the boarded covering of the walls. It smelt faintly of glue
and bales of material, as do all theatre workshops. And I was
standing there, waiting for the roof to fall in; wishing that it
would.

The young man, after an endless moment of silence, got
quickly to his feet. 'Well, I'll be getting back to the theatre
now. Thank you for the tea, George.' The great glass door
opened and closed, and feet clattered down the two flights of
iron fire-escape to the cobbled yard.

'Not your afternoon, Angus,' said George.

'God, but that must have been Olivier,' I said, knowing the
answer only too well.

'But I'd only just introduced you. Whatever possessed you?'
said George.

But George was wrong. It *was* my afternoon. Another step
had been taken in my long flirtation with the stage. I had met
Laurence Olivier.

'But what shall I do, George?' I asked. 'I should think there
is little you can do,' said George, with some relish.

I suppose insulting one young actor won't matter particu-

As a toreador, 1919.

As Hamlet with Michael Redgrave as Laertes, 1937.

As Victor Prynne with Noël Coward as Elyot Chase in *Private Lives*, 1930.

As Sir Toby Belch in *Twelfth Night*, 1937.

As Henry v with Jessica Tandy as Katherine, 1937.

As Iago in *Othello*, 1938.

As Heathcliff in the film of *Wuthering Heights* (Emily Brontë), 1938.

As Hotspur in *Henry* IV, Part I, 1945.

larly, I said to myself miserably, trudging tealess down St Martin's Lane, through a threatening pea-soup fog to Leicester Square and home to Acton on the Underground.

I will write to him, I said. Surely he couldn't think that I could be so gratuitously rude to someone I had just that moment met. So I wrote trying to explain and got his reply back directly.

He had been startled, he said, but after the first shock – amused. After all I had only voiced what all London theatre-goers were saying: but it was a little unnerving straight in the face. At any rate, I deserved to suffer the play in its two variations and here were the tickets. Four stalls. I was stunned. Of course I went and thought it wonderful, but I didn't 'go round' after.

I didn't meet him again until the brilliant 1936–7 season at the Old Vic. By then I had really become a photographer, although, as yet, I had had few commissions from the theatre companies themselves. However, I had perfected a method of getting my camera into any theatre where the play interested me. I would write and say – quite without truth – that the *Sketch* had commissioned me to photograph their show and could I come and take twelve shots. It never failed, and as the *Sketch* very often published the results I was never found out.

So here I was on the stage of the Old Vic waiting to photograph Larry and in *Hamlet*, and all three for the first time – the first of so very many occasions: I was to photograph thirteen different Hamlets, but there is no doubt in my mind which was the best.

Larry looked astonishing in the part; he had shaved the hair at the sides of his forehead and plucked his eyebrows, though I didn't realize this at the time. He had also painted the depth of his eyelids, that is the thickness down from the lashes to his actual eyes, with white, an old ballet trick, very startling; but more strangely still he had drawn a faint line under his eyes that started at the tear ducts and ran down over his cheek-bones. When I commented on this he said, 'Oh yes, tired boy stuff, don't you dare remove it with your bloody retouching, old boy.'

He is always wonderful with make-up, putting endless trouble into creating a special effect for photographs, the full stage paint toned down in a subtle way to fool the camera, even with the old man make-up for *Titus Andronicus* many years later. So much in contrast to Michael Redgrave's method of using his face as if he were engraving a copper plate, fine lines running in every direction; wonderfully effective from the audience, which is of course the whole reason for the exercise, but certainly very difficult for the photographer.

Then came *Twelfth Night* with Larry in an extraordinary make-up as Sir Toby Belch – the first of a long line of performances in the smaller character parts that have given me a superb collection of pictures.

It was the great parts that I loved photographing: Henry v, Coriolanus, Macbeth – he looked wonderful in the later scenes of *Macbeth*, with a head like an ageing lion. When I took the pictures round to his dressing room in the interval he had stripped off the heavy felt Motley clothes and stood there, naked, while his dresser sprayed him with eau de Cologne, looking with his white whipcord body like some medieval lad in a huge carnival lion mask.

Also in this season he played far and away the best Iago I have ever seen to Ralph Richardson's Othello – I suppose the story about that production is too well known to repeat, but here goes. I wasn't there, but it must have gone something like this:

Tony Guthrie: 'I say, Larry, I think I have stumbled on a possible explanation for Iago's odd behaviour. I think he must have been in love with Othello.' Larry: 'But what a marvellous idea, Tony! Can't we play it like that?' 'I don't see why not.' 'Let's do it then, but we mustn't let Ralphie know!'

It would be fruitless to make this a list of Larry's plays, simply because I have photographed them. Other people will talk about them. I can't do so in any constructive manner as I am no critic, and in any case I can't be critical where I love. But when Larry went to Chichester he took me there, and all those memorable productions under his management I photographed. Then I followed him back to the Old Vic, now the

National Theatre, and photographed his opening production of *Hamlet* with Peter O'Toole – not, alas, my favourite production of that play, and I rather disliked what it looked like.

Many other productions I photographed at the Vic, but always with some difficulty. In a busy repertory theatre with only one stage and rising costs it was difficult to give me the stage time necessary to produce my kind of work, quick though I am, and I had to resort to a lot of snapshooting – a type of photography, I feel, that almost anyone can do. But I stuck to it for the pleasure of working with him as an actor, and under him as a producer, and in the end I got my reward – I was asked to photograph *Othello*, which made all the difficulty and frustration worth while. Not that I was ever given the stage for any length of time, but I was given it for short spells and was able to use my big camera for a few shots. It is interesting that these are the shots of the show that are always used.

But what a thing to photograph – the best Shakespeare production I have ever seen. Not that the settings were all that good photographically and, excepting in the first and last scenes, it never looked very exciting; at least, not to a photographer and not to me. But I had great performances to photograph – at least three – and, oddly, great performances can be photographed as such : a ham performance will produce ham pictures.

Sir Michael Redgrave

LOGAN GOURLAY : The first time you appeared with Olivier was in 1936 at the Old Vic when you played Laertes to his Hamlet. Were you immediately aware that he was destined for greatness as an actor?

MICHAEL REDGRAVE : It's tempting to say that I was. But it would be dishonest. The truth is that I thought he was a bad Hamlet – too assertive and too resolute. He lacked the self-doubting subtleties the part demands. Every actor, even one as gifted and versatile as Olivier, is limited in his range of parts by his own temperament and character. The very boldness of Larry's personality, his natural drive and his pragmatism make him unsuitable to play an introspective, wavering character like Hamlet. Michael MacLiammoir once summed it up when he was talking about actors like Larry playing Hamlet and he said: ' I never quite trust these pragmatic minds. They don't see the mystery and the poetry.'

Still, although I wasn't impressed by his Hamlet at that time I could see that he had what Noël Coward called ' star quality '. There was nothing small or petty about him as an actor or as a man. Whatever he did was on the grand scale. In fact I became aware at that time that he liked the same scale in everything around him. I remember going to a christening party for his son Tarquin at his home, which was an enormous studio in Chelsea with enormous windows, and enormous fireplaces – a setting that would have dwarfed lesser men; but he was very much in his element.

Our tastes are dissimilar and our temperaments are different but despite this – or maybe because of it – we became friends

68

during that production of *Hamlet* and we have remained friends ever since.

LG: But it was a long time after *Hamlet* – over twenty years – before you acted together again.

MR: Yes. For some reason we never found ourselves in the same cast – not until 1962, when he invited me to join him in the opening season of the Chichester Festival Theatre. The first production, *Uncle Vanya*, turned out to be a really memorable one. Unlike that early *Hamlet* the casting was right. He played Dr Astrov, a character he understood perfectly, and I was Vanya, a part that would have been unsuited to his talents and temperament.

At the beginning of rehearsals I was reminded of his pragmatic attitude. I had to miss a Saturday morning rehearsal because my daughter Vanessa had invited me to her wedding to Tony Richardson. She wanted it to be a quiet affair with absolutely no publicity so I couldn't announce the real reason for my absence. Instead I left a message giving the first excuse I could think of, which was that I had a grumbling appendix.

After the wedding I received a telegram from Larry telling me I should have a colonic irrigation and that he had arranged an appointment for me with a Harley Street doctor who specialized in this treatment. I forgot all about it the following week, and as we got immersed in rehearsals I never had an opportunity to give Larry an explanation about the wedding and my appendix. But he didn't forget, and a little later I got another telegram saying: 'You naughty boy. You didn't keep the Harley Street appointment. You are still unirrigated.'

LG: What did you think of him as a non-medical, stage director?

MR: He was constructive and concise. Always considerate to his cast. During rehearsals actors can be sensitive – perhaps over-sensitive – and if they are criticized by a director in front of their colleagues they can easily lose the confidence and assurance they are trying to build up. With his actor's experience Olivier was specially aware of this, and if he had criticisms to make as a director he always took the actor aside and did it quietly.

However there were one or two occasions when he forgot this golden rule. One of them occurred when we were doing a run-through of *Uncle Vanya* at Chichester. When it was over he turned to his wife, Joan Plowright, who was playing Sonya, and said: 'Darling, you're like a little girl from Scunthorpe doing an audition for RADA.' Then he focused on me and said: 'Very good Michael, but loud echoes of Sir John. Very loud echoes.'

But that kind of director's bitchery is really uncharacteristic of him. I can remember only one other occasion when he indulged in it and that was when I joined him for the opening of the National Theatre in 1963. I played the King under his direction in the first production of *Hamlet* with Peter O'Toole. After one of the rehearsals Larry said to me: 'When you played Macbeth you made a marvellous first entrance. You strode on and you looked as though you were saying to the audience: "Fuck you all. I *am* Macbeth." Now when you come on you look as though you're apologizing to the audience.' I took this rather badly at the time and I suppose I sulked a bit. Characteristically, Larry forgot all about it and weeks afterwards he said to me in the dressing room: 'Michael, what have I done to offend you?'

I'm afraid that in more ways than one that *Hamlet* wasn't the most satisfying production for me. The sets, which were by Sean Kenny, may have looked impressive but they created difficulties for the cast. For example, one of the reasons for my apologetic entrance was that I had to stoop and pass under a heavy archway before I faced the audience for the first time. It's not easy to look commanding or regal just after stooping. Then later in the play Larry had directed me to make a move that I could never do without looking unnatural because of the positioning of part of the set. During the run he sent me a note saying that by his count I had got the move wrong at least seventeen times. I was reminded of the time in Paris when I was being directed by Orson Welles and I could never get one of the lines right. Welles finally said: 'When a good actor keeps getting one of the lines wrong there must be something wrong with the line. There's only one thing to do – change the line.'

Unfortunately the sets and that move in that opening production of *Hamlet* at the National were never changed and it remained an unhappy experience for me.

LG: Have you been impressed by what the National has done since then?

MR: Yes indeed. Apart from that inauspicious start I think it has been an outstanding success, despite all the difficulties facing such a project. And there is no doubt that the success is largely due to Larry. For him, establishing the National has been the fulfilment of a long-cherished dream. No other man of the theatre in this country could have done it. He is that very rare amalgam – the actor and the administrator, the artist and the manager.

LG: What do you think have been his greatest achievements as an actor?

MR: First of all I should like to say that within his range – which is by no means narrow – he has few, if any, equals on the contemporary stage and he will undoubtedly take his place with Garrick and Kean in the pantheon of great English actors. But even when he has ventured outside his range – in some film parts, for example, as well as in *Hamlet* – he has never failed to reveal some interesting and unexpected aspect of the character he has been playing.

If I were asked to name his greatest Shakespearean performance I should find it difficult to choose between his Othello and his Richard III. In modern plays I think he gave virtuoso performances in Ionesco's *Rhinoceros* and in Osborne's *The Entertainer*. Incidentally, he himself told me recently that his own favourite part was the Captain in Strindberg's *The Dance of Death*, because he felt that the character was closest to his own.

I should have thought myself that his own character is too

complex and subtle to be captured and delineated in one part, even by a Strindberg.

LG: What would you say if you were asked to sum up his character in a sentence or two?

MR: It could only be done in a series of apparent contradictions.

I remember I won the *Evening Standard* drama award in the same year as his wife, Joan Plowright, and at Larry's request we received the awards in our dressing rooms instead of being fêted at one of those grand luncheons. I overheard him saying to one of the reporters: 'I don't really approve of all these awards for actors unless I'm receiving them.' It was said in jest, of course, but there may have been an underlying truth. He can be fiercely egotistical and at the same time he has great humility. But that's a fairly common contradiction in brilliant artists. In his case there's also pragmatism and imaginativeness. Flexibility and obstinacy. Sensitivity and ruthlessless. Idealism and practicality. And a few others.

But then it's only the small men of lesser talents who can be easily and neatly categorized.

Harry Andrews

LOGAN GOURLAY: When did you first meet Laurence Olivier?

HARRY ANDREWS: It was in 1936 when I was asked to play Tybalt in *Romeo and Juliet* at the New Theatre. As Romeo Larry caused quite a stir. He decided to go for realism and play him as a full-blooded passionate Italian youth without caring too much about the poetry. This interpretation worried Gielgud as director and there were quite a few arguments during rehearsals. But fortunately there was no serious clash.

LG: How was Olivier's Romeo received?

HA: The critics weren't very pleased. I remember one of them said: 'His blank verse is the blankest I've ever heard.' And another wrote: 'He played Romeo as though he were riding a motorbike.' But the public reaction was much more favourable. I myself thought it was a very exciting, bold performance. So was his Mercutio. We had a duel scene to do together in this production using two-handed swords and buckler with dagger. He liked to do this realistically too and we used to slash away at each other every night as though we really meant it. Hardly a night passed when we didn't do each other some damage. He likes to say he still bears the scars to this day.

LG: Did you think then that he was going to have an outstanding career on the stage and become our leading actor?

HA: At that time Gielgud was unquestionably the leading actor on the English stage, though it was beginning to be obvious that Larry was going to rival him. But I'm not sure that Larry himself was convinced he would rise to the very top. He was ambitious but he never gave the impression that he was completely dedicated. He didn't seem to take himself too seriously. And he didn't think he had always made the right decisions about his career.

LG: Why?

HA: Well, some time before *Romeo and Juliet* he'd been in the original production of *Journey's End*. But he'd turned down the chance to do it when it opened at the Savoy and became an enormous success. Instead he decided to do *Beau Geste*, which he thought would give him more scope, but it was a flop. A colossal flop. Then there had been the Garbo disappointment. He had accepted an offer to go to Hollywood and appear with her in *Queen Christina*. But he didn't make the right impression on Garbo and he was asked to leave just after the film started. John Gilbert, one of her old leading men, took over, I think.

LG: Did he ever talk about these mistakes and disappointments?

HA: Not a great deal, except to make fun of himself, which was characteristic of him. He certainly didn't brood about them. Incidentally, I appeared with him in a few charity performances of *Journey's End* after *Romeo and Juliet*. And then I didn't work with him again until after the war.

LG: Did you have any contact with him during the war?

HA: Not until nearly the end. I was in the army and he came to Germany in 1945 with the Old Vic Company, which included Ralph Richardson and Sybil Thorndike. They were doing *Peer Gynt* and *Richard* III. It was a wonderful experience for me to see this brilliant ensemble playing. I had to drive over a hundred miles with my troops in lorries to get there but I'd have gone ten times the distance after nearly six years of theatre starvation. I went round to see Larry after the performance and he said: 'Let me know whenever you get out of the army and there might be an invitation to join the company.'

LG: Did you get the invitation?

HA: Yes. Fortunately I got out shortly after, towards the end of 1945, and I went straight to the Old Vic, taking over the parts from George Curzon. I think that was a more frightening experience than any I'd had during the war. I had to face three first nights in a row – in *Oedipus* and in Parts One and Two of *Henry* IV. I don't think I'd have survived without Larry. After so long away from the stage I was jumping in again right at the deep end but Larry, thank God, saw me through. He went out of his way to help me, though he had quite a lot on his own plate. With the *Oedipus* he was doing Mr Puff to bring the curtain down. It was a *tour de force*. The stylized, mannered comedy of Mr Puff in *The Critic* immediately following the deep tragedy of *Oedipus*. They went mad about him in New York when we went over there in 1946 for a limited season. We also did *Uncle Vanya* in that season with Larry as Dr Astrov. Another remarkable performance. I think he had reached his first great peak of sustained achievement at that time.

LG: What did you think of his Lear, which was done the following season at the Old Vic?

HA: It wasn't a complete success but it was by no means a total failure either. He directed it himself and that perhaps was too big an undertaking. But parts of his performance were fascinating. There's a lot of comedy at the beginning and he brought that out brilliantly. But he just didn't have the vocal guns at that time, particularly for the storm scenes. Still, he had tremendous presence. I'll never forget how he looked when he did his 'Howl, howl, howl ...', standing there with Cordelia, supported just on one arm. Majestic and moving.

LG: Do you know why he never tackled Lear again?

HA: Combination of circumstances. He always wanted to try it again I think, but there was always something to prevent him. I believe he was planning to do it not so long ago at the National, but his health wouldn't allow it. It's a terrific physical strain playing a part of that scale. But it's a great pity he hasn't been able to do it again. Vocally, he'd be all right now. His voice has got much more depth. He's always said he's a tenor, but he's learned over the years to extend his range. He's done it of course in many other non-vocal ways. He's never been content to concentrate all the time on Shakespearean and classical parts, demanding as they can be. He's always been eager to find new challenges, try out new ideas on the stage and the screen.

LG: What do you think of him as a screen actor?

HA: He's a master of the technique of screen acting, though I suppose he's never been a big box-office star in the Hollywood sense. But it's not something he wanted to be, and anyway it's seldom related to great acting. I don't think anyone has succeeded as well as he has in putting Shakespeare on the screen, with the exception of that Russian *Hamlet*. It's always been one of my great regrets that his plans to film *Macbeth* never came off. He wanted me to play Macduff. After leaving the Old Vic I hadn't worked with him for some time, except for a season in New York when I joined him in the two Cleopatras – 'Two on the Nile' as they called it – which he had been doing under his own management at the St James's. When we came back from New York he told me he had a wonderful script for *Macbeth* and he was very keen to do it. They did a lot of preparatory work, including a trip to Scotland to find the right locations. But then the bottom fell out.

LG: What happened?

HA: He couldn't get the financial backing. Some film he'd done hadn't been a great success at the box-office, so the money boys backed down. I still think it was engineered in a way to get him to do another film he didn't want to do. He was told he had some kind of contractual obligation and he was forced to go into *The Devil's Disciple* with Kirk Douglas and Burt Lancaster. He insisted that I should have a part too, because I'd given up other offers to leave myself free for *Macbeth*. It was a nice gesture and characteristic of Larry, but *The Devil's Disciple* turned out to be an unhappy film for everyone concerned. Right from the beginning the atmosphere was bad. Larry was still angry about not being able to do *Macbeth* and naturally resentful about having to do something else. The atmosphere went from bad to worse during shooting. He was treated disgracefully, I think. It's the only time I've seen him lacking slightly in confidence, though when it came actually to doing it in front of the cameras he came over better than anyone, as he always does.

LG: Which of his Shakespearean films did you like best?

HA: The *Henry* without any doubt. It was probably the most suitable for screen adaptation, and it was more rewarding visually than the *Hamlet* or the *Richard*. But the *Macbeth* might have been the best of all. I think he still regrets not having done it. It must have been one of the few occasions in his career when he was unable to do what he had set his heart on. Usually he lets nothing stand in his way.

LG: Do you mean that he can be ruthless?

HA: Ruthless would be too strong a word. Single-minded I'd say. Single-minded in doing what he thinks is right for him professionally. But that's part of the equipment of all men of great achievement — that kind of single-mindedness. They decide what they want to do, and they do it. However in his case I don't mean he does it regardless of everyone else. There's a story that illustrates this in a way. I hadn't appeared with Larry for some time and I don't think I'd seen him for nearly a year. It was 1958, I think, and suddenly out of the blue one Friday he called me up and asked me down to his country house, Notley Abbey, for the weekend. I said I'd be delighted to go. Naturally I was looking forward to seeing him again and I particularly wanted to get his advice, because on the previous day Glen Byam Shaw had called me up and asked me to go to Stratford for the following season to play Coriolanus. Well, when I told Larry about the offer on the Sunday over drinks he said, 'Marvellous, you must do it.' I pointed out that I wasn't sure if I'd be right for it and anyway Glen must have asked him to do it. Larry replied: 'Well, as a matter of fact he did ask me about six months ago but I turned it down. However, now I think it might be a good idea.' So I then said: 'In that case, Larry, you must do it.'

LG: Did he agree immediately?

HA: Not immediately. When I spoke to Glen after the weekend he still insisted that he wanted me finally rather than anyone else, but I rang Peter Hall, who was going to direct, and said: 'Surely it would be very exciting for you as director to have Larry in the part?' and he replied: 'If you put it that way the answer is yes.' To cut a long story short, I bowed out – as I thought I had to in the circumstances – and Larry played Coriolanus, but I was given another good part in the production. There was no bad feeling. In fact we stayed together at the Welcome Hotel in Stratford during rehearsals and the work went very well. He was having a difficult time personally. His marriage to Vivien Leigh was breaking up. But he gave a great performance. In a way it was absolutely right for him to do Coriolanus at that stage in his career. So to sum up he had made the right choice for himself – and for the theatre.

LG: Do you think he's always been right when he's made what you'd call a single-minded choice?

HA: Not always. There's another story further back in his career about the casting of *Lear* in that 1946 season at the Vic. The three directors at that time were Larry, John Burrell and Ralph Richardson. When they sat down to discuss what they should do John Burrell said: 'I think we should do *Lear*. Now which of you would like to play it?' I think his intention was that Ralph should do it. He was the more obvious choice then. However Ralph said: 'Why don't you do it, Larry?' – probably not meaning it at all. And Larry said: 'No, you must do it, Ralph' – not meaning it either. Finally, of course, it was Larry who did it and Ralph played the other big part that season, which was Cyrano and which would have been more suitable for Larry. Still, the results were by no means bad. Each gave a very interesting performance, though Larry, as I've said, wasn't quite ready for Lear and Ralph wasn't as good as Cyrano in the physical aspects – the sword play and so on – as Larry might have been.

LG: What do you think has been his most memorable stage performance?

HA: It's difficult to select one from so many. I'll always remember his Hotspur, which he played in the forties. And his Coriolanus. But I'm forgetting his Richard III, which combined all the things he'd done so well in other parts. It had everything – the comedy, the irony and the tragedy too. In the non-Shakespearean parts I think his Captain in Strindberg's *Dance of Death* was brilliant. He got his effects with great economy. But probably his finest outside Shakespeare was his Dr Astrov in *Uncle Vanya*. Quite beautiful. Then in contemporary plays he was outstanding as Archie Rice in *The Entertainer*. It was a virtuoso performance. The way he did the swift changes of mood was remarkable.

LG: What would you say has been his least successful part?

HA: Let me say first of all that I don't think he could ever give a really bad performance. Or a dull one. Whatever he does on stage has something interesting and compelling about it. But perhaps his least successful performance was in a contemporary play called *Semi-Detached*. He was playing an ordinary provincial man and he got the accent perfectly – a Nottingham one, I think – but the play didn't give him enough scope. It was a bad choice. I don't know what made him decide to do it except that it was contemporary. One of his faults is that he tends to worry too much about keeping up with the times. I don't mean that he's trendy or anything like that. But he's sometimes too concerned about falling behind the times and being thought old-fashioned. Still, that probably led to his doing *The Entertainer* and, as I said, that was a *tour de force*.

LG: Has he any other faults that affect his work?

HA: I may be misjudging him, and others, but I don't think he has always picked the right people to advise him and work

with him off stage. Too many of them have been mediocrities –
not really in his league.

LG: Do you think that has applied at the National Theatre?

HA: In some cases, yes. Of course he's done a magnificent job
himself getting the place established and running it, but I'm
not sure he has selected the best team to help him. Still, I'm
not suggesting for a moment that he's surrounded himself with
' yes men '. He's much too intelligent for that. And besides, he's
much too self-critical. He'd see through any silly sycophancy.
He's never really satisfied with what he's doing. Not so long
ago when I was filming in *Nicholas and Alexandra* with him
in Spain he had a very difficult emotional scene, which he did
quite beautifully in one long take. He played it with absolute
true emotion and with real tears – yes, real tears, which he
doesn't always produce. I was right next to him and as soon
as they said, ' Cut ' I told him I thought he'd been great. But
he said : ' No, I was too weepy. A bit too weepy. I'd better have
another take.' So he had another take.

LG: Hasn't he always been critical of his own physical appearance?

HA: Very much so. He used to think he wasn't tall enough so
he wore elevators on stage, though he's a good height – just
under six feet. And right up to his middle period he padded his
calves and thighs in costume parts, because he thought his legs
were too thin. He took up weight-lifting to build himself up,
and he became quite thick-set. I think he still does some weight-
lifting to keep fit. When he was young he thought his hair-
line was too low and he shaved it back. And he's never liked
his nose, so he's never missed an opportunity to play around
with false noses. He takes infinite trouble with make-up. He's
in his dressing room long before the curtain, meticulously pen-
cilling in lines – lines that the audience may not see – whereas
someone like Ralph Richardson will stroll in much later and
get the effect he wants with a few bold strokes. Another worry
of Larry's is that the backs of his hands are ugly. I don't think
they are, but the point is he does, and that's why – as you'll

have noticed – when he's doing an emotional gesture he shows the palms of his hands. Of course it's been very effective and he's made what he thinks is a defect into an asset.

LG: Do you think he has any unfulfilled ambitions?

HA: I think he'd like to do the Lear again, but it may not be possible. He's had his great disappointments, like not being able to film *Macbeth*. But all in all he's had a long and, I should have thought, a very satisfying life, on and off the stage. I remember years ago as we were driving up to Stratford together when we were doing *Coriolanus* he said: 'Well, now my baronial period is just about over. I'm not sure what comes next.' He was talking about his life at the country house, Notley Abbey, and his married life with Vivien Leigh. He enjoyed living there in great style and he did a lot of work himself in the grounds planting yew trees and fussing about the hedges. Now, I suppose, he's in his Regency period, living at Brighton, and of course professionally it's the National period. Whatever else he does the National will be a monument to him. When the new building opens on the South Bank I think one of his biggest ambitions will be fulfilled. He deserves the greatest credit for what he's done. I can't think of anyone else in the country who could have done it.

Douglas Fairbanks Jr

First meeting? Can't remember. New York? London? Hollywood? Transatlantic liner? Just can't remember. Was it 1930? or 1931? or 1932? All the old snapshots of the period could have been taken anywhere. Perhaps he knows. I don't. I do remember though that, despite a fine start on the London and New York stage, Hollywood in those days thought him no more than 'promising'. He was married to Jill [Esmond] at the time, and it must have been frustrating when her movie career got started more conspicuously than his own. He was then, as he remains today, very convivial, capable of hilarious impulses, and an ever-willing, good-natured collaborator in his own victimization in what now seem to have been some rather damn-silly legpulls, perpetrated by his small coterie – of which, let it be confessed, I was one. He was serious about his work, but little else. We, his early Hollywood friends, had considerable respect for (and envy of) his wider professional experience, but we were shamefully at pains to disguise it, notwithstanding our firm and open affection for him.

There are lots of examples of our juvenile jokes. Take, for one, that deep-sea fishing (?) trip down the Pacific coast, when some of us persuaded the local constabulary of a tiny Mexican village to arrest 'good old Larry' on the sole charge of his being an Englishman; and when he frantically demanded to see the British Consul, the giggling *policia* told him that Mexico didn't recognize Britain. And then the other time when we paid an ex-prizefighter-stuntman $5 to burst in on the poor innocent chap's dressing room and loudly threaten him with every variety of mayhem for having made off with his non-

existent wife. At the time it was all very ha-ha-ha-ho-ho-ho!
But, in retrospect, it's just so many shivers.

3 September 1939
Weekending on a chartered yacht off California's Catalina
Island and anchored in the yacht-club harbour. . . . Let's see,
there was Larry and Vivien (they weren't yet married) and, as
a chaperone, Viv's mother . . . and Niven . . . and Walter
Kerri-Davies . . . and Bob Coote . . . and Mary Lee (my wife)
and me. Chamberlain was on the radio from London. . . . War
had begun with Germany, again. . . . We listened grimly, each
concerned with special thoughts of his own. The silence was
finally broken, and not, as might have been expected, by the
usually ebullient Niven, but by Larry – of all people! Without
our noticing it, he had quietly and unobtrusively proceeded to
get as smashed as a hoot-owl. Then, very solemnly and carefully, he had climbed into a dinghy, and rowed away. On
reaching the stern of a fairly large anchored yacht young
Laurence stood up, just steadily enough not to fall into the
water, and, like some Cassandra-in-swimming-shorts, bellowed
to all within earshot: 'This is the end! You're all washed up!
Finished! Enjoy your last moments You're done for. . . .' Before
the bemused layabouts could reply our Larry-boy was again
rowing resolutely off to the next yacht that caught his bleary
eye and repeating his prophecy of doom. . . . An hour later an
official protest was delivered from the club's secretary, not to
us, but to the owner of a small sailing yacht close by, demanding an immediate apology for having insulted other club
members. The owner was Ronald Colman. I decided it was time
for us to weigh anchor and get the hell out to sea. . . .

William Wyler

1938: I arrive in London to do the casting of *Wuthering Heights*. Ben Hecht had suggested Laurence Olivier. Fortunately, I had seen him in a play in New York. Samuel Goldwyn, the producer, and I agreed he was the best choice. We met several times at Larry's house, where he and Vivien Leigh lived. So I presented what I considered a 'plum' for any actor, particularly one relatively unknown in America. But Mr Olivier was less than enthusiastic, though he agreed that it was a good script, and that Heathcliff was a good role.

I assumed his reluctance was due to a previous unpleasant experience in Hollywood, until he took me one night to see a film in which Vivien appeared. This was in fact a subtle suggestion that I might use her in the film as well. She was excellent in what I saw. Fortunately, there was Isabella, a secondary role, not yet cast and later played by Geraldine Fitzgerald, which I immediately offered her – and which she immediately rejected. 'I will play Cathy,' she said. Ah, but Cathy was already cast with Merle Oberon, who was an important star in America under contract to the producer. 'I will play Cathy or nothing,' she said. I tried hard to persuade her. Since she was still unknown in America, I assured her that she could never get a better part than Isabella in her first American film. Deathless prophecy!

Larry and I had some difficulties in the early days of *Wuthering Heights*, for two reasons, I believe. One was a lack of communication and articulation on my part; the other was due to Larry's unfamiliarity at the time with film acting, having worked mostly on the stage. In a subject as passionate and Victorian as *Wuthering Heights* the line between getting the

most or too much out of a scene is very thin. But how gratify-
ing for a director to get from the actor the maximum in performance, often more than is expected, or required, never
having to 'coach' him to heighten a scene, only occasionally
nibble away a bit. I believe his portrayal of Heathcliff is the
most important single contribution to the success of this film.
We ended up good friends, a friendship I value highly, though
regretfully we don't see each other but about once in ten years.

While I was serving with the United States Air Force in
England in 1943, Larry asked me to direct *Henry v*. I told him
I didn't know Shakespeare well enough, and he said, 'Never
mind; I know Shakespeare, you know film-making. Together
we'll make a fine picture.' Well, he did make a fine picture, a
splendid one, not with me, but alone. I don't know if he asked
any other directors, but after I declined, I can see him saying:
'To hell with these –.' No, he is too polite for that – even
talking to himself – so he probably said, 'Blast these directors.
I'll direct it myself.' And so he did. And bloody damn good,
too!

After the war it was my turn to offer Larry a film. So we
made *Sister Carrie* by Theodore Dreiser. I believe Olivier's
Hurstwood is the truest and best portrayal on film of an
American by an Englishman. He used to spend evenings with
Spencer Tracy just to hear him talk. But the film was not a
success. I was told it was too grim. During the shooting Larry
asked me why I was making this story into a film. Obviously,
he had little faith in it. And he was right. The public stayed
away *en masse*.

The director who gets Laurence Olivier to play a role in his
film is fortunate indeed. A first-rate performance is assured
and a matter of course. Little directing is required, except for
technical matters. The characterization has been thoroughly
studied and well conceived and will be thoughtfully and effect-
ively performed. The director need worry only about how
best to put it on film. He can devote more time and effort to
the other members of his cast and to the many other aspects
of film-making. More than that – he can get some additional
help if he can use it (and who can't?). Since Larry is interested

in every phase of the film in which he appears – not only his own share – expert advice, sharp and honest critical opinion (hard to find) are available for the asking. Besides, the director need never worry as so many have so many times: 'Will he show up today? Will he be sober? Will he know his lines? Will he want to rewrite the scene? Will he try to direct the lighting – or the other actors? Will he insist on being photographed from his "good side" only? Will he ask for a late call or an early dismissal?' Laurence Olivier does not indulge in this kind of old-fashioned nonsense. He is too professional, too disciplined and too good.

Some stars could learn a great deal from him, not only about acting but also about how to act when not acting.

Merle Oberon

'This actor is the ugliest actor in pictures. This actor will ruin me.' One's wildest imagination could not lead one to believe that these words were directed at Laurence Olivier. But they were. This used to be the highlight of one of Larry's favourite Hollywood stories.

During the early days of the shooting of *Wuthering Heights* Larry had unnecessarily acquired athlete's foot. We were shooting the film in sequence, and had filmed three days with Larry as the stable boy in our initial scenes. Sam Goldwyn strode on to our set on this particular day, and called cast and crew around him. Larry was on crutches because of the athlete's foot, and it took him somewhat longer to gather around than most. As Larry put it, he made a splendid picture of 'the show must go on' – the brave actor coming to work despite discomfort and crutches.

The attention he expected was at least a pat on the shoulder for his courage. Instead Sam, with a face puce with fury, and pointing an accusing finger at Larry, cried out in a voice that undoubtedly carried to Sunset Boulevard, 'Thees ector es the ogliest ector in pictures, thees ector will ruin me.'

Larry's mimicry of Sam's voice and manner were hilarious. What had caused this panic in the hierarchy was Larry's make-up, and appearance in general. He had insisted on looking like an authentic and very grubby stable boy. Coming from the Old Vic, where he had an enormous success, he didn't agree that he should tone down his make-up and performance for the magnifying screen. He was finally convinced by seeing the rushes of the first few days. It is really interesting to look back and realize we were witnessing a great actor adapting his art from stage to screen, even though we all suffered a bit from the growing pains.

I was essentially a screen actress, and though only twenty-two at the time was treated like an old shoe. I don't believe William Wyler, the director, looked at me too much; though I do remember he did make a suggestion in the death scene. I had to cry with happiness at seeing Heathcliff, combined with a sense of frustration at knowing I was leaving him. After the first take Willie said: 'A little more [tears] in the left eye.' I occasionally still tease Willie about this, and we have a good giggle. But the results of Larry's performance are now notable in the prouder annals of the history of motion pictures. The film itself (in spite of the old shoe) is in the archives of the Library of Congress of the United States Government.

But *Wuthering Heights* was not an easy film to make. We had our troubles. I caught a cold that threatened to develop into pneumonia, so in the scenes where Cathy has to search for Heathcliff in the rain, Cathy was forced to wear what skin-divers call a wet-suit under her silk dress, the rain had to be warmed, and Alice, my stand-in, had to bear most of the storm.

Another point (for which we still get criticized – especially by the British) was the height of the heather. Our excellent set designers had built an extraordinarily convincing Yorkshire landscape in Chatsworth, a suburb of Los Angeles. We were due to film the love scene in the heather on a Thursday. While running down the hill I sprained my ankle, so the scene was postponed until the following Monday. The heather, already the height of Yorkshire heather, had been planted on Wednesday for shooting Thursday. On Monday, when we arrived to do the scene, you could hardly see me for the heather. No one had reckoned on the power of the California sunshine. Larry and I ran through what looked like extremely healthy wheat. People still say – in the middle of telling me how much they liked the film – 'But how come they didn't know that heather doesn't grow that high?'

Alexander Knox

If, in the old days, you wrote a popular song about love in June the obligatory words were 'above' and 'moon'. In a piece about Lord Olivier it is as obligatory to say he's the best actor in the language.

Such a statement might be considered adequate by some, but not by Lord Olivier. He'd want to know how, why and in what way. His chief complaint about Willie Wyler when that subtle and poetic man was directing him in *Wuthering Heights* – there were many complaints and I remember them clearly because I was Lord Olivier's guest at the time and he would frequently come home from the studio frothing at the mouth – was that Willie wouldn't tell him what was wrong: seventy-two takes of one scene and not a word of comment in between them. Miss Merle Oberon was gracious, obliging and 'professional'. Lord Olivier was fit to be tied.

His communicable but ineffective fury was indicative of three things: his particular genius in his trade, his desire to understand what he was doing and, most important, his desire to be understood, not so much by the public as by people who knew. I think he's always had the notion that there *are* people who know. If I'm right about that I'm afraid I disagree with him profoundly. In my opinion the things you can know about have to do with craft or talent, the things you can't know about have to do with genius.

(In my opinion, and as you see in parenthesis, this is the secret of much of the fine film Willie Wyler has produced – he has encouraged, not always by the obvious or the most agreeable means, the operation of genius. He has not been satisfied with a display of talent.)

Lord Olivier, in my opinion, has always set greater store by his craft and his talent than by his genius. This lack of confidence has always surprised me. Many lesser actors have more. His craft and his talent are great: in the class of Chaplin. His genius is superb: in the class of Chaplin, Garbo and Judy Garland. But his genius has been less vividly displayed. I think he's always been afraid of it. He's probably right. His genius, unleashed, could blast both cinema and theatre wide open, and audiences by the million would trample thousands to death as they ran quivering away to hide in some dim safe place, far away from lightning and other dangerous forms of illumination. (For that to happen, of course, he'd have to have the right play and the right part – I suggest Lucifer in a Cinerama version of *Paradise Lost*.)

If anyone feels that I'm writing high falutin nonsense I make the apology that there is no other way to speak of the higher reaches of any art without residing at Pseuds' Corner. An art on that level can be spoken of only in terms of parable and analogy. The only claim I make is that my parables and my analogies mean something.

And acting is so much the most involved and involving, subtle, intricate, intellectual and – it goes without saying – powerful of the arts that nine critics out of ten (if there are that many, which I doubt) can deal with it only by dissection. Dissection is a scientific technique or method appropriate when dealing with the dead. When dealing with a living thing it must, by its nature, alter and possibly destroy the phenomenon it ostensibly seeks to understand. (The real motive, Sean O'Casey seems to suggest in *The Flying Wasp*, is destruction, not understanding, but he may be wrong.)

What is unfamiliar frightens us. We often feel that what frightens us must be destroyed. Genius, in any art, has to do with the unfamiliar. Craft and talent have to do with the familiar. Lord Olivier, had he allowed himself to be governed entirely by his genius, would have found his career destroyed and, quite probably, himself as well. Seven out of the ten best actors I've seen in my lifetime have died of drink. This is a high mortality rate even for an industrial disease.

Working critics will, of course, disagree with me, and I have some sympathy. You can't buy groceries with semi-metaphysical meanderings. Editors, on the whole, prefer understandable material. Working critics must, unless they dare to become, occasionally, a Coleridge, or have the brains to become, occasionally, a G.B.S., concentrate on appearing to understand that which cannot be 'understood' in that sense; or on proving themselves capable, brilliantly, of appearing to make clear what the artist has preferred to leave, at best and deliberately, translucent. The best of them presume to reduce it, in simpler words, to dimensions capable of being understood.

(And what else am I doing now? It's an old argument. If we think of all art as a sort of masonic job producing blocks of a certain shape and kind in order to build a certain house – quite probably a house not seen before – the critic incorrectly assumes that he is helpful when he detects and reveals the dimensions of each block, its weight and composition. Two questions at this point: one, can he convey the feeling of the house by describing the blocks of which it is built? two, if he can so accurately define these subtleties why the hell doesn't he build the house?) The fact that he doesn't seems adequate proof that he can't. Once a critic loses reverence he loses relevance. And no critic of the theatre with deep reverence has come to my notice since Desmond MacCarthy.

It's vulgar and unappreciative of me to admit it, but there's no escaping it. My chief admiration for Lord Olivier is for the manner in which he has preserved, with integrity, a measurable quantity of genius in a world that prefers his talent.

Leo Genn

I can think of no one – no one at all – of whom I find it more difficult to give an objective appreciation than Larry Olivier.

In the first place, he is, in my view (which I know is shared by a great many people), the Leading Man of the Theatre in the fullest sense anywhere in the world today, and that term embraces the stage, films, television and any other medium that one can think of. As actor and director, his achievements in film and the theatre in particular are absolutely monumental.

Secondly, I certainly owe my postwar good fortune in theatre and film – certainly the major part of the opportunity to achieve it – to Larry's absolute insistence, to the point of virtual folly, that I should play in the film of *Henry v*.

Thirdly, profession apart, as a friend he ranks as high as anyone I can think of, and when I talk of friendship in this connection I am referring not merely to good companionship or *camaraderie*, but to the kind of relationship that admits of no real barriers, and which happens only a very few times, in my experience, in one's whole life.

That I was able to play in *Henry v* at all was indeed one of the small improbabilities, among a very great number, which added up to the total improbability of such a film being made at such a time (1945) when shortages were at their worst, personnel unavailable, bombing continuous and every sort of difficulty to be added to those inherent in such an undertaking even at the best possible time. Larry, Vivien, my wife Maggie and I had been used to meet on most leaves. He was by that time back from Hollywood and serving in the Fleet Air Arm at Portsmouth; on one leave he told me he was going to be released to make *Henry v* and that, if he did, I must play the Constable of

France, which indeed I had done at the Old Vic, with him and directed by Tyrone Guthrie, in 1937.

At that time I had, in fact, played the Constable of France and the Duke of Burgundy, not as a 'double' but simply saying on the programme, 'The Duke of Burgundy, Constable of France' and cutting out the line that referred to the killing of the Constable at Agincourt. In the event, of course, it wasn't possible to do this in the film, since there was a hand-to-hand battle between Henry v and the Constable, which resulted in the Constable's death. All that in parenthesis, however, since I replied that it would be utterly impossible as, at the time it was suggested, I was in fact commanding a training battery and we were just starting the build-up of training gunner regiments for D-Day something like a year later. However, Larry was not prepared to take 'no' for an answer from me or, as it transpired, from the War Office, who said a definite 'no' when he asked for my release. After many discussions, however, he said: 'Has he not got any leave due?' to which the reply was: 'Yes, twenty-seven days'; he said: 'Very well, can't he do the work during his leave?' To this they agreed (after reference to my commanding officer) on condition that I did not do more than three days at any one time. This would have been quite enough to make anyone in his right mind say: 'Well, that's impossible,' and forget it, but not Larry, who chose, if you please, to so schedule things that I was able to come down overnight from Shropshire, where I was stationed, do three days' work, go back overnight and be with my battery on the following morning parade. Hence my reference to the utter folly of my being so employed.

Incidentally, those completely crazy few days on *Henry v* provided at least two absolutely first-class examples of Larry's very special talents as, if I may refer to such a thing in these days, an 'actor's director'. In this particular regard he ranks in my experience with Rossellini, and ahead of anybody else I have ever worked with, even including people of the calibre of John Huston and Anatole Litvak. The quality, in particular is that of never saying a word if a gesture or an indication would help in itself, never using one word more than is necessary to indicate what is wanted and, in Larry's case, saying: 'Can I show you what I mean?' only in the last resort. The two things I have specifically in mind are simple enough. The first occurred on my first morning of shooting (the first time I had been on a film floor for something like four years). I was, understandably perhaps, even more nervous than one usually is on the first day of a movie, certainly less practised and relaxed. The scene was set at the French court, with Harcourt Williams as the French King, surrounded by his four main courtiers all draped round in our own particular poses. Just as we were ready to shoot Larry passed me on the way to the camera, put his hand under my chin and raised my head with a jerk. That was all; he said nothing and did nothing more but it served to make me stand erect, physically as well as mentally, and was all I needed to start me off in a proper frame of mind, instead of in a nervous, doubled-up, restricted way.

The second instance occurred in the tent scene, which I had played for comedy, though this is not traditional or usual. It concerned the two lines when the messenger comes in and says: 'My Lord, the English lie within 1,500 paces of your tent' to which the answer is: 'Who hath measured the ground?' He replies: 'Milord Grandpre', and the reply is: 'A valiant and most worthy gentleman.' I played it for a double laugh, as I had done years before on the stage, and the scene was done in pretty big close-up. At least four times Larry said: 'Fine, but make it less', until finally I made it nothing at all, in my judgement, at which he immediately said: 'Fine, print it.' I said: 'But, Larry, for heaven's sake, I did absolutely nothing; there won't even be one laugh, let alone two'; and he just looked at me and said: 'I know what you think, but will you kindly just wait for tomorrow's rushes and then bloody well see if I'm not right.' And, of course, he was.

Peter Glenville

LOGAN GOURLAY: Did you ever work with Olivier when you were a young actor?

PETER GLENVILLE: No, but I met him and got to know him when I was playing opposite Vivien Leigh in *The Doctor's Dilemma* at the Haymarket. That was during the war and he'd just been released from the Fleet Air Arm because the authorities thought, quite rightly, he had a contribution to make to the national effort as an actor.

In a sense at that stage of his career he was a frustrated actor because he hadn't played the big parts he wanted to play. I don't mean he blamed the war for interfering with his career. On the contrary he was very patriotic and he had volunteered for service. I think he had felt the same way before the war: in his view other actors whom he considered no better than himself had been given more opportunities to tackle the big classical parts. So he was resentful and a bit envious.

You could say that he was unnatural, unaverage in the sense that all great musicians, artists and actors are unnatural because of their fierce concentration on their work. Compared to the ordinary man with ordinary ambitions Larry was a deep-sea monster. He thought about nothing but the great classical roles and how he wanted to play them.

He also wanted to appear with Vivien Leigh because he was very much in love with her. But his love was second – a close second, but still second to his obsession with acting the great parts. He didn't have the lesser ambitions that befog the issue. He didn't want to make a lot of money and he didn't want to be a filmstar. Although he would welcome affluence he didn't concentrate on it. Although he would welcome headlines he didn't seek them. His only ambition was to be a great classical actor.

LG: Do you think he had any doubts about succeeding in his ambition?

PG: He must have had doubts at times because he had encountered lots of discouragement. I remember his first night at the Old Vic two days after Lilian Baylis died when Michel Saint-Denis directed him in *Macbeth*. Some of the critics said he lacked the equipment for classical acting. In particular they said he didn't have the voice; one of them described his voice as a 'thin trumpet'. He was advised to go back to being a matinée idol and concentrate on plays like *Design for Living* and *The Green Bay Tree*, in which he had been very successful.

With all his charm and romantic good looks he could have continued to be successful in that sort of play, but he was determined to do Shakespeare and the classics even after the failure of *Romeo and Juliet*, with Vivien as Juliet, in New York. It was a total disaster. I believe the notices were so bad that the public actually queued up to get their money back.

At that time, particularly after his success on the screen in *Wuthering Heights*, he could have gone to Hollywood and been a big, highly paid moviestar. He could have done the same at other periods in his career but he never wavered in his faithfulness to the classical stage. In fact when you think of some of the setbacks and discouragements he had, his tenacity of purpose was remarkable. Apart from talent, which he undoubtedly has in large measure, his tenacity – single-mindedness, determination or obstinacy, if you like – ensured his success.

LG: Although you got to know him well in his early and middle career it wasn't until you directed *Becket* in New York that you worked with him.

PG: Yes, I socialized with him, talked with him, argued with him over the years, but we didn't work together until *Becket*. Then shortly afterwards I directed him in the film *Term of Trial*.

As Justice Shallow in *Henry* IV, Part II, 1945.

As Oedipus in *Oedipus Rex* (Sophocles), 1945.
As Mr Puff with George Relph in *The Critic* (Sheridan), 1945.
As King Lear, with Alec Guinness as the Fool, 1946.

As King Lear, 1946.

As the Duke of Altair in *Venus Observed* (Fry), 1950.

As Antony with Vivien Leigh as Cleopatra in *Antony and Cleopatra*, 1951.

With John Mills and John Gielgud rehearsing for *Stars at Midnight*, a charity performance at the London Palladium, 1953.

As the Grand Duke with Vivien Leigh in Rattigan's *The Sleeping Prince*, 1953.

With Marilyn Monroe and Richard Wattis on the set of *The Prince and the Showgirl*, the film version 1957.

What was extraordinary was that when we did *Becket* he was then established as a great actor, if not the greatest actor on the English stage, and he had successfully directed several productions himself, but he never tried to take over in any way or even suggest what I should do as director. From my point of view he was the ideal. First of all he had all the technical equipment to do whatever was required. I could have asked him to play it this way, or that way, *à la française* or any way, and he would have been able to respond. He welcomed direction. Unlike all the young actors of today he would even ask me to give him a reading on a line. Because he thought I had a certain facility with readings – different ways of interpreting or emphasizing lines – he'd suddenly turn to me and say: 'I'm not too happy with my reading, let's hear another.' Funnily enough, this didn't mean he was losing confidence as an actor. It meant the opposite, because he knew that whatever the reading he could accept it and make it his own, modify it or broaden it – or just discard it.

Nowadays the young actors from the modern schools don't believe in readings. They believe in happenings, or visceral events. If you give them a reading they scream and say they don't even want to hear it. But Larry has such command of his craft that he could listen to any suggestions – any variations in interpretation – and make use of them if he wanted to. That's real professionalism.

Another indication of his professionalism was his concern and tolerance for the rest of the cast, particularly the small-part players. One of the problems, especially in New York, where the reserve of small-part players is much more limited than in London, is not only their competence but their impertinence – their bloody cheek. We had one example of it in *Becket* with a young actor who, when he couldn't get work on the stage, had been doing a little bricklaying on a building site. I had cast him as a mad radical monk and he had one scene with Larry. He should have felt enormously privileged to be on the same stage as Larry after a spell of bricklaying, but at the dress rehearsal he stopped dead after one of Larry's lines and didn't answer. So I shouted: 'What's the matter? Why

don't you answer and carry on with the next line?' He said:
'I haven't been given the right cue.' When I said: 'You've
been given an approximate cue,' he replied: 'Either the man
gives me the cue. Or he doesn't give me the cue.'

I was outraged, but Larry took it quite calmly. He was just
amused. However on the opening night with the same young
bricklayer-actor playing the monk Larry made a marvellous
transposition of words. His line should have been: 'This
monk has been found wandering about the camp.' Instead he
said: 'This camp has been found wandering around among
the monks.' It stopped the show for a minute and the bricklayer-actor was convinced Larry had done it deliberately, but
I don't think so. My experience of him in that production was
that he was enormously generous and tolerant to the younger
players even when they were impertinent. I've heard since
that he has developed an intolerant streak towards his colleagues but I find that difficult to believe. There was certainly
no sign of it during *Becket*.

LG: Anthony Quinn played the part of King Henry in the
production, didn't he?

PG: Yes. Larry had wanted to play the King but it was a New
York production and it would have been difficult to cast Becket
over there, so Larry – very generously again – allowed me to
persuade him to play it with Tony Quinn taking the showier
and more extrovert part of the King.

LG: Quinn and Olivier came from very different schools and
backgrounds. How did they get on together?

PG: Tony had a great desire to strike up a close relationship
with Larry. But Larry didn't encourage it. He was polite but
cool. He was professional but he didn't invite any 'rapping'
sessions.

LG: What are they?

PG: Mutual confessions. Probably derived from *rapport*. You
spell out your hates, loves, fears, frustrations and so on. You

spill it all out and unburden yourself. Larry is a fairly reticent man and he was having none of that. However they got on quite well together, but as you say, they came from very different schools and occasionally it was obvious. As you know, Henry and Becket have a close relationship in the play, with Henry saying: 'I love you, Thomas. You don't love me etc. . . .' At one stage during rehearsals Tony turned to Larry and said: 'My God, Larry, I hope they're not going to think that we're sodomites – a couple of buggers.' Larry smiled thinly and said: 'My dear chap, I hope they do. Didn't you know that in the Middle Ages at the time of the play all the men went at that kind of thing hammer and tongs?' It took Tony a moment or two to realize that Larry wasn't being serious.

LG: There's a story that may be apocryphal about Quinn being greatly impressed by Olivier's speech delivery and enunciation and asking him how he had achieved such standards. According to the story Olivier told him that in Brighton, where he lived, he walked about the beach declaiming Shakespeare with his mouth full of pebbles like the Greek orator Demosthenes. So Quinn immediately sent to California for pebbles and walked about Broadway with a mouthful, spouting lines and almost choking himself.

PG: It's a marvellous story but I'm afraid it is apocryphal. Tony did know, however, that he needed speech direction and he took it willingly. I had to teach him all the boring things that are part of the basic training in England but are not taught in America at all, like not joining a consonant to the next word's vowel and so on, but I'm afraid we didn't include the pebble method.

I must say in fairness to Tony that he finally made a good Henry – bold and powerful. Of course he could never have played Becket. When he had to leave to make a film Larry, with his wide range, was able to take over the part of Henry, which he had wanted to play in the first place, and we brought in Arthur Kennedy as Becket for the rest of the run.

Throughout the run Larry in both parts was the perfect professional. There wasn't one moment when he was tiresome, difficult or temperamental. There are very few stars of whom you can say that after a long run in which they played two challenging parts in a demanding play.

There was a good example of his professionalism right at the beginning. We opened cold in New York with only a few previews and after the first or second I realized that the play had to be cut. Our version was shorter than the original French production, which had run for about four hours, but we were still about twenty minutes too long. So I went home, made the cuts and next day gave them to the cast. Larry didn't make the slightest complaint. He didn't say, as so many stars would have done : ' I love that line or that passage. You can't possibly cut them.' Or in the circumstances, with so little time before the opening night, he would have been justified in saying : ' I cannot accept any cuts at all without upsetting the whole balance of my performance.' But he didn't. He simply took the notes about the cuts and that night we did the cut version. His professionalism was immaculate.

LG : Later on you directed the film version of *Becket* with Peter O'Toole as Henry and Richard Burton as Becket. Why didn't you cast Olivier in one of the parts ?

PG : Most people don't realize that at the time the play was set Henry and Becket were very young men. Henry was only twenty-two and Becket was thirty-four. Now on the stage, with the theatrical artifices to help, they could be played by older men, but in front of the film cameras it would have been difficult, even for an actor of Larry's talents, to drop so many years convincingly.

LG : Not long after the Broadway production of *Becket* you directed Olivier in the film *Term of Trial*. It wasn't an outstanding success. Do you know why ?

PG : No. Sometimes the reasons for success or failure defy analysis. The film had all the right elements. In addition to Larry playing the schoolmaster we had a good cast – Simone Signoret as his wife and Sarah Miles, whom I'd found in Worthing Rep., playing her first film part as the schoolgirl. Larry gave one of his low-key performances, which I always prefer on the screen. Though the film didn't turn out to be a great success we had an interesting and happy time during production.

LG: Did you find it more difficult to direct him in a film than in a play?

PG: No. Once again he was thoroughly professional and un-temperamental. He never quibbled or interfered.

Naturally one trims one's sails as a director according to the talents and experience of the actor. With a young, inex-perienced actor I will tell him how to gesticulate, or turn his head, or how long to hold a pause. But obviously with an actor like Olivier I wouldn't presume to offer my elementary direc-tion. After a scene I might offer some general observations such as: 'It seems too long', or 'too heavy' or 'too light', and we might do another take. Of course with positions, movements and camera angles I would say precisely what I wanted and that was never questioned.

LG: From your point of view as director did you find him con-structive? Did he ever make any suggestions?

PG: No, he didn't suggest anything verbally. His suggestions came in performance. He wouldn't have a theory and want to discuss it endlessly with you as director. He'd make his contri-bution by showing you in performance what he had in mind – a new emphasis or nuance, sometimes a whole new dimension. And $9\frac{3}{4}$ times out of ten you'd say as director: 'Brilliant. We'll keep that in.' But even if you said: 'It's good but it's maybe a little over the edge', he'd accept, and change accordingly.

LG: How did his film technique compare with his technique as a stage actor?

PG: In the first place he's a born actor. It's difficult to compare and measure his techniques in the two media; he's highly skilled in both. However I'd always say the man is a natural theatre actor rather than a natural cinema actor. But I think that's true of any great actor. A great actor wants to act, which he has more freedom to do on the stage. He doesn't want to worry about mechanical things, as he has to do in the film studios, like how near the camera is or how the lighting will affect him.

In *Term of Trial* there was one big speech in court when Larry had to defend himself against the accusations of the girl played by Sarah Miles. It was a long, two- or three-minute, speech – a great tirade. I decided I'd got a great actor so I wouldn't bother about tricky angles, close-ups and lighting effects as I might have done with a lesser actor to give the impression of a tirade. I simply said to Larry : ' I'll get the hell out of the way and let you get on with it.' I had two cameras – one in middle long shot and the other in medium close-up. I didn't use full close-up because the effect would have been overdone when he really pulled all the stops out. We did the scene twice and used the first take. He was great.

LG: Is there one performance of his that you consider his greatest?

PG: First of all let me say that no matter how pleasing and successful some of his film performances have been I wouldn't include any of them, because, as I was saying, a great actor's business is not on the screen and I don't consider him a film actor *par excellence*.

On stage it's difficult to select one from so many great performances, but one of the greatest – if not the greatest – was his Richard III with the Old Vic at the New Theatre. More recently his Captain in *The Dance of Death* was remarkably powerful. One of those performances that stays in the memory for ever.

I am always impressed by the fact that he can get up and give a gloriously rococo performance in a Restoration comedy like *The Recruiting Officer*. It's not so much that one of these performances stands out more than another, but the fact that after his Richards, Macbeths and Lears he can then do a superbly timed comedy of manners really shows how remarkably wide his range is.

Among the contemporary plays *The Entertainer* gave him his best opportunity and he took it brilliantly. I missed him in

Semi-Detached as a provincial salesman but I gather it wasn't one of his successes. There's a great danger when, like Olivier, you have played the great classical parts – mostly kings, princes and so on – that you find it difficult to get down to the level of ordinary life in a part. I'm not saying this was true of Larry, because I didn't see the play, but I suspect he may have played a great actor playing an ordinary man in the provinces. I understand he got the accent – Nottingham or whatever it was – perfectly. Of course he's always very interested in a cerebral, calculated way in the superficies of a part, like the accent. That doesn't mean that he's not interested in the deeper aspects; but he's an extraordinary perfectionist about the make-up, the accent, all the external features of the part. As a great craftsman he'll go to any lengths to get everything right and I can imagine him, for example, putting on or taking off weight for a part, whereas an actor like Charles Laughton, for instance, was always too fat but stayed that way and left the rest to the imagination.

Of course Larry will exercise the audience's imagination, too, but he's terribly concerned first of all about having all the physical details correct, particularly the facial details. I remember that once in *Term of Trial* he said he thought one scene should not be played with the sharp eye of someone who knows what's happened but with an air of perplexity – with a dead eye.

This puzzled me because, as I pointed out a moment ago, he didn't usually discuss what should be done – he simply did it. But then I discovered he'd heard that someone connected with the film had said that in close-up he had dead eyes. No actor likes to have that said about him, particularly one of Olivier's stature.

He may have suspected that I had said it and to find out he made that comment about playing the scene with dead eyes. But I was completely innocent. However what he does have, which could be confused with dead eyes, is a sort of tragic anaesthetization of feeling when the eyes go balefully dead. But it's a marvellous effect, not at all the same as having dead, expressionless eyes.

LG: In almost all of his big performances he produces a physical effect that's very striking – the cry in *Oedipus*, the fall in *Titus*, the epileptic fit in *Othello* and the dance in *The Merchant of Venice*. Did he introduce one in *Becket*?

PG: Not when he was playing Becket. It would have been unsuited to that part, which is quiet, cool, and cerebral. But as Henry he contributed not one particular moment, but an enormous overall physical energy, which was electrifying on occasions but never seemed excessive. I welcomed it as director.

You can almost touch his virtuosity and emotionalism at times because there's so much energy behind them. And at the same time he has, as I have said, a cool, calculated approach to the superficies of a part. It's an extraordinary combination – a rare amalgam.

LG: Sybil Thorndike says that Olivier is the greatest comic actor of the age but that he hasn't excelled to the same extent in tragedy. She thinks this is related to his own temperament and to the way he reacts to tragedy in his own life. He laughs it off: he'd die rather than submit to it.

PG: I don't mean this in an ugly sense, but I think that a great artist, musician or actor like Olivier has big, healthy appetites, among which is greed – greed for achievement. Larry certainly has that. He wants to shine; he wants to prevail. He doesn't have the quiet inner, philosophical resources that would make a tragic actor. I imagine, for example, that the temperament of a Duse would convert even a minor melodrama into a major tragedy because of a certain deep pessimism and irony in her point of view. But Larry has always been, even in his more mature years, a very alive, competitive animal with an optimistic zest for life.

At the same time I should say – and this may be due simply to my lack of experience – that I have never seen a great tragic actor. I don't think Larry comes off badly compared with any of his contemporaries that I've seen. I think John Gielgud is a superb romantic actor – a master of romantic pathos, sadness, with superb articulation and aesthetic awareness; but to a modern intelligence that's not tragedy. The nearest I've seen recently to total tragedy was Peter Brooks's *Lear* with Paul Scofield. I don't think Scofield achieved the total tragic dimension but the production did. It achieved what I consider in a modern context to be tragedy, and Paul abetted it superbly.

To a modern eye tragedy has got to be very firm, unsentimental, unromantic and profound intellectually – a very difficult thing to bring off, and if it's done at all nowadays it's done by a director.

Every age has its standards and degrees of tragedy. When you think of what's happened in ours it's very difficult to decide what a contemporary audience will consider tragic. Sybil Thorndike was right of course in saying that Olivier's ability to play tragedy, like any other actor's, is related to his own temperament, but she should have added that it's also related to the temperament of the age.

Another point is that if tragedy requires you to be introverted you must not be too subjective and esoteric. Now Tennessee Williams's *Outcry*, which I directed on Broadway, is a desperate personal cry – a *cri de coeur* from a highly talented and special man. But it's not tragedy because it's not universal enough. It's too subjective, too concerned with his own hang-ups and complexes. It's poetic drama of a high order, but it falls short of tragedy because it's so personal. This is a point that Sybil overlooks. Even if an actor has the tragic temperament it's got to be of a type that's related not only to himself and his inner problems, but to the age and time we live in, before it can generate real tragedy. That's a tall order, even for an actor with Olivier's range and depth of talent.

LG : Although you have spent most of your professional life during the last ten years in the States and you have not been associated with the National Theatre, do you have any views about its development under Olivier's directorship? Do you think, for example, as several people have said, that it would have been better for the Theatre and for him if he had concentrated on acting and left administration to someone else?

PG : It would be presumptuous and impertinent of me to comment since I've no first-hand experience of what has been going on at the National. I've had several conflicting reports from professional associates and it's impossible for me to judge who is right. I've heard that he has become intolerant and ungenerous on occasions with his colleagues, but I must say, as I mentioned earlier, that I find that very difficult to believe. As to whether or not he should have taken on the job of running the theatre as well as playing the big parts, I can only say, as I also mentioned earlier, that he has a greed for achievement and acclaim – an appetite for leadership. I don't think anyone could have stopped him.

Margaret Leighton

LOGAN GOURLAY: I believe you were discovered – if that's the word – by Laurence Olivier when you were a young actress at the Birmingham Rep. in the early 1940s.

MARGARET LEIGHTON: I don't think discovered is the word – at least not in the Hollywood sense of a star being discovered. What happened was that I'd been at the Birmingham Rep. for years and I think they must have been getting awfully bored with me. I was earning as much as I was likely to get there – about £9 a week, I think. One day Reece Pemberton, who was the designer, said, 'You can't get much further here. Why don't you go to London?' I said I didn't know anyone in London and he told me I should get in touch with a man called John Burrell who was at the BBC, and who was involved in forming a new company for the Old Vic. I wasn't very hopeful – I didn't even know much about the Old Vic in those days – but I did write to John Burrell and he asked me down to the BBC for an interview.

I didn't think I'd made much impression at the interview but a week later I got a telegram from him telling me he was coming to the Saturday matinée with two friends and asking me to book three seats. We were playing Pirandello's *Six Characters in Search of an Author* and we were getting a certain number of laughs. But came the matinée and no response. It was like the grave. I couldn't get a single laugh and I thought: 'My God, that man Burrell is out there with his friends and he'll think I'm hopeless.' I didn't know that his friends were the celebrated Laurence Olivier and Ralph Richardson, and of course what was happening was that the audience was staring at them and paying no attention to us on the stage.

However, the celebrated couple came round afterwards and to my astonishment asked me to join the company. I said I couldn't because I had another play to do at Birmingham. However they arranged to get me released and I did go, fortunately.

LG: Your first appearance with the Old Vic and Olivier was in *Arms and the Man*, wasn't it?

ML: Yes. We rehearsed it, I remember, at the National Gallery. It was 1944, towards the end of the war, and the last of the flying bombs were buzzing around. Larry was playing Sergius and I was Rowena – a part that I didn't understand at all. It's a difficult part at any time, and of course the bombs didn't help me to concentrate. Anyway I struggled through, wishing at times I'd never left Birmingham.

The two big productions in that first season were *Peer Gynt*, in which Larry played the small part of the Button Moulder, and *Richard* III.

I'd done some Shakespeare at Birmingham but I was scared stiff about appearing in *Richard* with the great Olivier. I was cast as Queen Elizabeth, not a very big or important part, but I didn't know how to tackle it. So I played safe, got the lines off like a parrot and bleated them out hoping for the best. In one of the scenes I had to sit on a throne bleating out my lines, which got more and more meaningless as the weeks went by. I never varied anything by an eyelash. I mean I even blinked on the same line at every performance. Larry got very fed up with me and he used to dash up to me on the throne, grab me and shriek his lines, trying to frighten me, I think, into a better performance. But I don't think even that did it. I'm surprised he put up with me. Still he did, and I survived, praying I'd improve the next season.

LG: Did you?

ML: Perhaps a bit. We did *Uncle Vanya*, *Henry* IV, *Parts One and Two*, and the double bill of *Oedipus* and *The Critic*. Looking back now I realize I was very lucky to be involved with the Old Vic and with Larry when they were doing such wonderful things, but at the time I was too young and inexperienced to appreciate it all fully. I just muddled through.

LG: How did he treat you, as a junior member of the company?

ML: He was never terribly grand and stand-offish. He could be very irreverent and down-to-earth at times. In the *Oedipus*, I remember, I used to be lying down on the stage with Vida Hope, moaning and chanting as part of the chorus, when he made his entrance. He wore a kind of abbreviated Greek kilt, a male mini-skirt, and as we writhed around peering up his kilt he'd say out of the corner of his mouth: 'Shut up, you old cows. You'd make a cat laugh.' It made us moan all the louder, and perhaps that's why he said it.

If I had to give my professional impression of him formed over the years I'd say that he can be ruthless and tough, but always in the interests of his craft or his art – always for highly professional reasons. In my experience he never wastes words and time doling out idle compliments. If you get a compliment from him you can be certain he's not just being kind to you because you look a bit miserable that day. He'd just let you go on looking miserable. He never praises you professionally unless he really means it. So I will never forget the few occasions – two to be exact, I think – when he gave me a word of praise. By the same token I'll never forget the moments when he has been cutting and critical. The first night of *Henry IV, Part One* was an example. In those days we had no tours or previews. It was repertory – at its best I think – and so it really was the first night.

The curtain went up at 7 o'clock or 7.30 and we had a dress rehearsal just before; that went on till about 6.30. At the beginning of the dress I did my little scene as Lady Hotspur with Larry as Hotspur, and then I went off stage and through the pass door to watch the rest of the performance from the stalls. I sat down just behind Sybil Thorndike, who was playing Mistress Quickly. Larry came through shortly afterwards and sat down with her. When she said something about me and the scene I'd played Larry said: 'Oh my God, the girl's a fucking parrot!' They didn't know I was sitting just behind, happily.

Well, I thought, that's that, the curtain's going up shortly and I'll just have to parrot along. I was in the dressing room getting made up when I had a summons from Larry. I went to his dressing room fearing the worst. He was sitting in front of the mirror intent on his make-up and he hardly looked at me as he said, 'Now, Maggie, how much of a memory have you got?'

I hadn't the wit or the nerve to say 'Like a fucking parrot's, darling!' Anyway he just went on and said, 'I've got some changes for our scene that you'll have to memorize quickly. Instead of entering left on the prompt side you must enter OP. I won't be downstage as I used to be. I'll be halfway upstage.' He told me I should go towards him and when I said, 'Lo, I cannot bear it', or whatever the line was, I should take a deep breath on 'bear it' because he said: 'I'm going to pick you up then. You're a big girl and I won't be able to do it unless you take a breath.'

Then he said he'd carry me about for the next three speeches and after that take me up on the throne and play the rest of the scene there.

I'm mentioning all this to show how painstaking and perfectionist he was. He worried about every detail and he'd make changes right up to the last moment, which is a very daring thing to do.

LG: Did you remember all his instructions?

ML: More or less I think, in my parrot-like way. Anyway the changes worked very well, and made the lines more meaningful. The whole production was a success, largely due to him. There was one moment in it which I'll never forget, and oddly enough it was a moment when he didn't seem to be doing anything. He just stood on one side of the proscenium arch and looked across at me. But what a look. I could feel the passion – the sex – coming over in waves. I've never felt that kind of thing so strongly in any scene with any other actor.

LG: Do you think the audience could feel it too?

ML: I don't know, but I imagine they could up to a point. He has amazing power – almost hypnotic. He can dominate an audience just by his presence on stage without uttering a line.

LG: He reached a peak of achievement in his acting career during those seasons at the Old Vic. What do you think were his best performances then?

ML: His Richard III was the definitive one. A remarkable performance. His Hotspur in *Henry IV, Part One* was outstanding, I think, and so was his Justice Shallow in *Part Two*. His Oedipus got a tremendous amount of acclaim but of all the parts he did then I liked it least. Not because of his interpretation or playing of the part; it's the part itself I disliked – the nature of the part; it's too grim and heavy for my taste. I preferred him in the romantic parts: as Astrov in *Uncle Vanya*, for example, which we did in the same season. I don't think he'll ever be excelled as Astrov. And I mustn't forget his Mr Puff in *The Critic*. That was a brilliant comic performance.

LG: It has been said that he has excelled more in the great comic parts than in the tragic ones. Do you agree?

ML: Speaking for myself I find it easier now to play something to make people laugh than to make them cry. However I think it's a mistake to put comedy into one rigid compartment and tragedy into another. They very often come together. It's an oversimplification to talk about great actors like Olivier and Richardson being greater in tragedy or comedy, because they can – and have – excelled in both and sometimes in the same part. When I was working with both of them at the Old Vic I had a tremendous admiration for Richardson's acting because it was immaculately truthful and immensely moving. Yet it was technically concealed and subtle – more than Olivier's was then, or so I thought. But that doesn't apply now.

It's a question of experience. As a young actress I used to think it was lovely to see someone ranting and raving on the stage, but as you get older you realize it's much better to put the lid on it – to get your effects with more discipline and control as Olivier does now.

Of course there are elements in acting – even at the top level – that are self-indulgent, but Olivier has learned not to be, except perhaps with his false noses and his acrobatics on the stage. He loves throwing himself about, taking great physical risks.

LG: He directed some of the productions when you were at the Old Vic. What did you think of him as a director?

ML: I think he's a brilliant director. The first thing he directed me in was the *Lear* during the third season – 1946 I think – when I played Regan. I knew nothing about *Lear* and he astonished me by having everything worked out in great detail. He explained his whole plan for the play, and in particular my part. He had planned every single move for Regan and each move was in accordance with the text and helped to explain it. So there was no question of asking, Why do I go there? Every move he gave me seemed to be truthful and right. He would tell me: 'When you say this line you're moving up there because you're thinking so-and-so.' He wasn't just getting me out of the way of somebody with a spear. It was a marvellously meticulous piece of direction, and at the same time he made me understand not just my own part but the whole play.

He did the same for me even in the other Shakespearean productions that he didn't direct. He made them completely real for me. He brought out the meaning in a way I hadn't heard before. It was an eye-opener for me. He got the sense – the dramatic sense – and the poetry took care of itself. I know he has been criticized for not paying enough attention to the poetry, but after all, if it's Shakespeare's poetry, it can take care of itself.

LG: Would you say he had a greater influence on your career than anyone else?

ML: Up to a point, yes. I certainly think he's one of the greatest actors I've ever worked with – if not the greatest. Unfortunately I've never worked with him again since those seasons at the Old Vic. We appeared in the same film not so long ago – *Lamb* – [*Lady Caroline Lamb*] – but we didn't have a scene together so we didn't even meet.

I don't think I'd dare to act with him now on the stage. I'm not indulging in false modesty. What I mean is that when I did act with him about thirty years ago I was raw and inexperienced. If I got off at the end of the evening without falling down and making a fool of myself I thought I was doing quite well. But now I'd expect much more of myself and to be faced with Olivier would be blinding. I'm not sure I could measure up to his standards. I'm more aware now of how high they are and I'd be afraid of looking inadequate by comparison.

I remember the first time I ever saw him in the flesh at the Birmingham Rep. I thought I was inadequate in another way. He seemed to have great physical appeal then and I remember thinking to myself, I'm too plain. I'd never be able to play opposite him in the kind of parts that Vivien Leigh has played. I couldn't match up to him in terms of glamour.

LG : Yet he once said in an interview that he looked like a weed as a young actor. Did you know that he was nearly forty before he appeared on stage in tights without padding his legs?

ML : I remember at the Old Vic hearing that for months before he appeared in that tiny Greek kilt in the *Oedipus* he went regularly to a gym for work-outs to build up his legs. I also heard that as a young actor he thought his hair line was too low and his nose wasn't right. Obviously the fact that he was so self-critical had something to do with his development and success. I mean if you start out at the age of twenty-two like a moviestar thinking, ' I look lovely, my hair line is perfect and my nose is dreamy,' then you don't develop as an actor and by the time you're thirty-two you've got nothing to offer but a fading profile.

One of Olivier's great strengths is that he's never been self-satisfied and smug about himself and his work generally. He's never sat back and said: ' Aren't I marvellous?' He's always been slogging away at something. If he thought he needed more muscle for a part he went to a gym. If he needed a particular accent for a part he studied the accent until he got it perfect. It's the old saying, I suppose, about genius being nine parts application and hard work.

He's also on occasions shown some of the humility that goes with genius. I remember hearing what he said about being fired in Hollywood when he'd gone out there to appear in *Queen Christina* with Garbo. He said: 'She knew everything about acting in movies and I knew practically nothing. I couldn't match up to her, so they fired me – and they were right to do so.'

LG: More recently he has been encountering criticism as director of the National Theatre. Do you agree with any of the criticism?

ML: I've heard all kinds of backstage stories and gossip – everybody in the business has – about Larry doing that or not doing this. But that kind of petty bickering is inescapable, I suppose, in that context. And what's it got to do with the price of eggs?

Perhaps running the National and playing principal parts is more than any one man can take on. Yet it's difficult to delegate – some people find it impossible. John Clements, for example, who followed Larry at Chichester, says he knows he does too much – organizing the season, directing and acting too, but he could not delegate. Perhaps Larry has had the same trouble and when he has tried to delegate he may have picked the wrong people.

It's difficult for me to judge. I've never played at the National, though I must say I'd like to one day. But I'm a bit frightened. I'm afraid I'd feel very much out of it. The people there seem to be such a closely knit group, and they don't seem to be terribly happy in their work. So perhaps there is something in the criticism of Larry's reign at the National. However at the same time I can't think of anyone else in the theatre who could have taken on the job and built up the National from scratch. He may have made mistakes but, my God, think of the achievements.

LG: You said earlier that he was one of the greatest, if not the greatest, actor, you had worked with. Is he the greatest for you as a member of the audience?

ML: He appeals to my intelligence more than any other leading actor, including Alec Guinness. And of all the others he is the only one who can be sexy in the best sense of that word. He can convey real passion. So he appeals more to my sex and to my intelligence than any other actor. He may not regard that as much of a compliment coming from me, but by my standards it is the highest.

Timothy Bateson

LOGAN GOURLAY: At the beginning of your career you had an unusual meeting with Olivier – at a concert wasn't it?

TIMOTHY BATESON: Yes, in the Albert Hall. I had been invited by Malcolm Sargent to use a seat in his box at an afternoon concert. When I got there I found that the other person in the box was Laurence Olivier. I'd just started my career as an actor and of course I was overawed, but at the end of the concert I summoned up enough courage to say to him, 'Excuse me, sir, I'd like to come and see you.'

I don't think he knew who I was, although we'd met briefly the year before, so he asked what I wanted to see him about. I told him I was an actor and that I'd like to join his company at the St James's. He made what I'd call one of his characteristic remarks, 'How very sweet of you'; and he gave me a phone number to call the next day. Of course I rang and after an audition I got into his company at the St James's. It was the Festival of Britain year when he presented the two Cleopatras with Vivien Leigh – Shaw's *Caesar and Cleopatra* and Shakespeare's *Antony and Cleopatra*.

LG: You said you had met briefly the year before. What was the occasion?

TB: I was the unknown visitor – or the gatecrasher – at his country house, Notley Abbey. What happened was that I was appearing at Stratford and an old friend of mine, Harry Andrews, who was also in the company, had been invited to Notley to spend a Sunday. Harry suggested that I drive him to Notley, go on to Oxford and then come back to pick him up a bit early in the hope that I might get a chance to meet the Oliviers.

My memory probably romanticizes it all a bit now but as I recall it, when I did get back to Notley I rang the bell and the door was opened by a dignified old butler called Trudgett. I really can't be certain now that there was a butler and that his name was Trudgett, but what was true was that Larry Olivier and Vivien Leigh made me feel very welcome. I remember he took me into the study and showed me Edmund Kean's sword and talked nineteen to the dozen about the theatre.

Later on in the sitting room with the other guests he suddenly stood up waving a record and said, 'Have you heard this new recording of Verdi's *Requiem*?' and slapped it on the radiogram. He partly conducted it and when it came to a passage he particularly liked he'd shout: 'Just listen to this bit. It's marvellous. Marvellous.'

I sat there like a schoolboy with my eyes popping out of my head. It was an experience I'll never forget. The setting was magnificent and everything was very theatrical – a bit larger than life. It was a glimpse into that period of his life when he and Vivien Leigh were very much the royals of the theatrical world and they lived accordingly. At that time I suppose he was coming towards the end of the royal period.

LG: But he was still very much on the throne when you joined the company at the St James's the following year.

TB: Yes indeed. I remember how terrified I was when I was told by the director to stay behind after a performance because Sir Laurence wanted to see me. I was playing the clown in *Antony and Cleopatra* and I'd been playing him for the first two weeks as a creaking old man of about ninety-eight.

Anyway to my great relief when I went to see Sir Laurence he was very friendly. He put his arm round my shoulder and said: 'My dear boy, if we had wanted O. B. Clarence (an old character actor) in this part we could have got him, but we decided to use you.' I thought to myself: 'Well he's being nice about it but I'm still about to be fired.' Instead he went on and said: 'I'd like you to imagine what would have happened if

Cleopatra had taken the worm and it had bitten her, but instead of dying she'd just been very ill for several weeks and then had recovered. I'd like you to think of her sitting in the garden of the palace one evening and her maid servants are talking to her and asking: "What was it like that night when the worm bit you?" And Cleopatra might have said, "I was very unhappy because of Antony and I was sitting on the banks of the Nile sobbing when suddenly out of the mist at the side of the river there came a young boy who didn't know I was a queen. He came and spoke to me and comforted me. He made me feel all was well and I might see Antony again. As he chatted to me I fell into a sleep."

'Now,' Olivier added, 'if you could give us that – if you could think of the clown as that young man – it could be very good.'

Of course I changed my performance as he suggested and the rest of the company, not knowing I'd had a talk with him, thought I was being very bold and imaginative. Anyway, the point was that the change worked very well and this gave me the confidence I needed. As a director he's specially good at inspiring confidence in his actors.

LG: And specially sympathetic, I imagine, to all their problems.

TB: Yes, of course. His great value as a director is that he can depend on his instinct – his actor's instinct – to tell him what will get over to an audience. However, it can be a bit disheartening working under his direction because he can always play the scene so much better than you. And there's a danger of saying to yourself, 'Why bother. I'll never be able to do it as well as he can.' But the right way to think of course is that you've seen the best and though you cannot equal it you can at least try. Then as I've been pointing out he knows how to make you feel confident. I remember years after the two Cleopatras being directed by him in *The Broken Heart*, one of the opening productions of the Chichester Theatre. My part was a small one but I had one fairly long speech and I was tending to rush it a bit out of nervousness. At one of the rehearsals he came tearing down the aisle through the stalls, leapt on to the stage and said: 'You must slow it down, dear boy. Remember when you're up here making a speech you're the only person that matters. Take your time. Show the audience you're confident. About 90 per cent of all acting is confidence.'

Of course it's something that has marked all of his own great performances – the sheer confident daring with which he will hold a pause, for example, linger over one word, or suddenly change the pace.

LG: Did you work for him between the two Cleopatras season at the St James's and the opening of the Chichester Theatre?

TB: Only briefly, unfortunately, in two films – *Richard* III and *The Beggar's Opera*.

LG: There was a gap of more than ten years between the St James's and Chichester. Did you notice much difference in him and his attitude to his work when you encountered him again at Chichester?

TB: Yes, a marked difference. At the St James's he was very much the leader of the profession, still in his royal period, as I said earlier. But later at Chichester he was much more the working actor and director. I can tell a story which illustrates this. On one occasion at Chichester during rehearsals for the opening we had to go to a civic reception, which was to be attended by all the local big-wigs. Before going Olivier gave us a little pep talk telling us that we should be on our best behaviour and that we should try to create the right impression. Then he added: 'There's just one more thing. Can anyone lend me a suit?'

He was in his rehearsal clothes – an old shirt and a pair of jeans – and, as he was living in Brighton then, he had no time to go home and change.

I thought back to an earlier occasion at the St James's when he rehearsed *Antony* wearing a morning coat and striped trousers because he had to go to some function at the Palace at 4 o'clock in the afternoon.

Now that change in sartorial standards may not be very

important in itself, but it's an indication of the change in his general attitude and scale of values. One of the most outstanding things about him and his career is how he has kept moving on from one phase to another. He has a remarkable ability to transcend the years and say: 'Well, that's the end of that chapter. I must move on to the next.'

Many talented men have ten-year spans of greatness in their chosen spheres. But usually as the world has moved on, they haven't. They're still great, but only within the context of their particular periods. Olivier is an exception. He has never allowed himself to stand still. He's always been seeking, and finding, new challenges. So he has sustained his career over several decades and he's still at the peak of his profession. Only a few years ago he tackled Othello, which at his time of life and in his state of health was a remarkably brave thing to do.

I know opinion was very divided about his performance but in my view it was a triumph. I think he succeeded, too, in the other Shakespearean part that, like Othello, is almost unplayable, and that's Macbeth. I've seen many actors fail at it but to my mind when he played it at Stratford in 1955 he was brilliant. Yet oddly enough it was a simple performance; he got his effects economically but commandingly.

LG: He has sometimes been criticized for the way he has spoken the verse in Shakespeare. What do you think?

TB: I'm not really sure what good verse-speaking is, particularly in terms of the stage. I know Gielgud can do it. But I don't know if his is the only way of doing it. Perhaps if you were able to listen to recordings of all Olivier's verse roles you'd come to the conclusion that his verse-speaking should be criticized. But Kean was often accused of mashing up the verse. Certainly Olivier did that to some of the verse in *Antony*. However, he did things in his performance, which I saw every night, that were pulverizing in their effect. The point I'm getting to is that I know actors who can speak verse beautifully but I wouldn't cross the road to see them as Antony or Hamlet.

Talking about poetry, it should be remembered that a performance can have a poetic quality that has nothing to do with verse-speaking or elocution. His performance in *Uncle Vanya* at Chichester had that quality.

LG: Were you disappointed when you weren't invited after Chichester to join the National Theatre company?

TB: Towards the end at Chichester I was given indications, as were many in the company, that there were possibilities for us at the National. I recall having an informal talk with one of Olivier's associates who described very loosely the structure planned for the National, in which I might fit. So without having had a definite offer I shouldn't have been surprised if I'd received a phone call saying: 'Come to the National.'

However the phone didn't ring and fortunately I had other irons in the fire so I wasn't terribly unhappy or disappointed. But naturally when the plans were announced I looked to see if I had been the only one of the Chichester company to be left out, and I discovered an almost complete change in personnel. Many of the new people had more associations with the Royal Court than with the main line of classical productions with which Olivier had been linked. Obviously he had decided to associate himself with the contemporary Royal Court influences, in the choice of productions as well as the style of acting, because he wanted to ensure that he wouldn't get bogged down in the past. It would have been so easy for a man of his age and eminence to carry on as before. But it wouldn't have been characteristic. He was determined that the National should have some contemporary relevance and that it shouldn't become just a theatrical museum.

LG: Do you think he succeeded?

TB: Yes I do. It seems to me that the National has been a triumph for him despite all the difficulties. And that he should have done it in the sunset of his career is a remarkable achievement. Of course he's made mistakes. Perhaps some of his associates were the wrong choice. He may have been influenced in some cases by the fact that they were young and *avant-garde* rather than by their basic talents. He may have listened to bad advice at times and followed it. But that shows, apart from anything else, that he's willing to take advice. He doesn't think he knows all the answers: he doesn't think he's God. He has a profound streak of humility.

I remember his appointment as director of the National was announced when we were at Chichester. That night we stuck a Union Jack on his dressing-room door with a message under it saying: 'God Bless, Sir.' When he came into the theatre and saw it he stopped outside the door, put his hands together, bowed his head and said, 'Please, God. Help.'

You may think that's just a rather mawkish little theatrical story. But remember he didn't know that one of us happened to be near at the time and to overhear. As far as he was concerned he didn't have an audience for once.

Peter Cushing

While making *Hamlet* there was a sequence where Hamlet, Horatio (Norman Wooland) and Osric (myself) walked down a spiral staircase. Technically this presented difficulties for the sound department, which resulted in the whole scene having to be post-synchronized.

During the interim period of a couple of months or so I had the misfortune to lose three of my front teeth through abscess poisoning, and by the time I returned to the studios for the post-synchronizing session I had been fitted with a plate that caused me a certain amount of embarrassed self-consciousness. Laurence noticed something odd about my speech, not present before, and winkled the reason out of me. 'You are afraid of spitting at people,' he said, putting his face within a few inches of mine. 'Drown me: it will be a glorious death so long as we can hear what you're saying.' Just one illustration of the many kindly and helpful suggestions he made during my long association with him.

I also remember that he and I were the only actors who used their own hair for *Hamlet*, his being dyed blonde and cut in the classical style with a small fringe in front; mine grown long – curling at the ends – not unlike the fashion favoured by today's younger generation. Laurence looked at us both in a mirror and remarked: 'We are the only two who look as though we're wearing wigs.'

One morning early I was in the make-up chair when he entered quietly, put his hand on my shoulder and said: 'I'm taking an Old Vic company on a tour of Australia. I'd like you to come along. Think about it.' I did, and the only thing that bothered me was the thought of being parted from my beloved wife Helen for nearly a year. 'I'll have none of that,' he assured me. 'There was too much of it forced upon most of us during the war. You bring Helen with you.'

So, of course, we went.

The people of Australia had done everything in their power to make us comfortable and at home. But as there were so very few real theatres in some of the towns we played in, the dressing-room accommodation was very limited. In Perth, I think it was, the auditorium was so large – it was normally a cinema – that Laurence, upon seeing the vast arena, said: 'We'd better dress up as Christians and throw ourselves to the lions.'

There were only two quite large dressing rooms. These had been beautifully appointed and decorated for Vivien Leigh and himself, leaving a few 'cupboards' for the rest of the fifty-odd personnel. However, they both insisted that their fellow mummers should share those lovely rooms while they made do with make-shift affairs comprising tables, chairs, screens and even inverted boxes in the wings of the stage itself.

Such was their attitude to all of us throughout that remarkable tour. *We* came *first*.

By this time he had received his knighthood and some amusement was afforded us by the uninformed, so understandably muddled by the Old Vic – Vic Oliver – and Sir Laurence Olivier – calling them Sir Oliver and Lady Leigh and even 'Old Vic himself'.

He once told Helen and me how lonely it was in his position where nobody would have the temerity to tell him how his performances were standing up to so much repetition (always an actor's worry during long runs). 'I wish they would,' he sighed, 'because we all need a sounding board and it's of no help to be told that you were "splendid" tonight, because you can't be – always.'

He had a wonderful knack of 'one-word' inspirations for telling other actors how to approach a character. To me 'Scout-master' for Britannus in Shaw's *Caesar and Cleopatra*; 'old-time movie' for his production of *The Proposal* by Chekhov (normally a half-hour one-act play which he 'speeded down' to nineteen minutes flat). One of these has bitter-sweet memories for me. He had cast me as a Free Frenchman in a play entitled *The Sword of Damocles* by Bridget Bolland and starring John Mills, which he was presenting at the St James's Theatre some time after we had returned from the Antipodes. My first entrance was preceded by a knock on the door, which I did with a normal 'rat-tat' and entered.

'Victory signal,' I heard him cry from the stalls. Exiting again I repeated my former knock and appeared once more. 'Haven't you heard of Beethoven's Fifth?' the voice asked. Whereupon I burst into tears and the whole episode ended in my having a nervous breakdown, which had been building up for several weeks; I suppose this very slight rebuke was the last straw. Immediately he was at my side, concerned and compassionate. I had to be 'off' for six months and receive treatment from a psychiatrist. From that moment on Laurence put me under contract, paying me a salary until such time as I could work again.

Christopher Fry

The first performance I remember seeing of Olivier's was the Romeo of 1935. One reason why I remember it is that I disagreed with the critics who attacked him for not giving full value to the poetry. For me, that slightly crackling delivery, flames starting up under a pile of new twigs, set the words free of 'tone' to do their own work. It may not have been the whole Romeo – no doubt the Mercutio was the performance to have seen – but what lyricism was lost was made up for by the exact life of the words, and this, after all, was what the poetry was based on.

Much later on (in the fifties was it?) when I saw his Macbeth at Stratford, I thought the quality was often overreached. Clarification had become analysis. It was as though he were taking a speech apart to show us its inner workings, and the sense of the speech stopped ticking as each glittering spring and cog was picked up by the tweezers and laid before us. So, for a time, I thought his real greatness was in comedy, not tragedy, in spite of the glorious summer of his Richard III (finer in the theatre than on film), which had its being midway between the two worlds; and in spite of the cry of Oedipus which still reverberates. What could outshine the twin brilliants (alas, I missed his Hotspur) of Puff in *The Critic*, tossing snuff into the air and nosing it down again, and Justice Shallow? Did I really see what I thought I saw, when Falstaff dragged Shallow full tilt from the orchard – Olivier horizontal in mid-air, his feet as high as his head? Such a piece of acrobatics is easier to recall than the playing of the lines. The shrivelled old Cotswold crab was simply there, living; and anyone who saw the performance 'will talk of mad Shallow yet'.

But any reservations I had about the tragic roles were swept away by the Othello. No performance of the greatest Shakespearean parts – of Hamlet, Othello, Lear – can be definitive, and it may be that 'the full soldier', the warlike Moor, was lacking, sacrificed to the dark and glowing panther. But I knew by the trembling of my body as I left the theatre that I had heard 'the hum of mighty workings'. The rage was elemental, the pain so private that it seemed an intrusion to overhear it. At the Old Vic, but not on the open stage at Chichester, 'But yet the pity of it, Iago! O Iago, the pity of it. Iago!', was whispered, face to the wall; and yet it was as large as torment itself.

I haven't seen the film, and so I can't say how much of what I saw is perpetuated there. I only know that I was present at a performance of superb stature.

By a mischance, I haven't ever seen him at work in rehearsal, though he directed the play *Venus Observed* he commissioned me to write for the St James's Theatre, and played in it. After the first reading by the assembled cast he asked if I would mind not coming to the early rehearsals. 'It would make me self-conscious,' he said, 'and I might show off instead of concentrating on the work.' The stage director would let me know when they were ready for me. But I didn't hear anything more, and so I spent my days at the rehearsals of *Ring Round the Moon*, and then went to Brighton for its opening there. On the day of the dress rehearsal at the St James's I rang up the stage-door to find out what time the rehearsal was due to begin. Olivier came on to the line. '*You're* a funny sort of author,' he said, 'never coming anywhere near us.' But after the rehearsal was over we spent a good part of the night talking about the play and the performance.

I gave him some anxiety about having the script ready in time. I had written to him to say that the second act was about to be posted off to him, but by then I was so far on with Act III that I thought I would wait and send them both together. A small parcel came from Olivier. It contained a typewriter ribbon, too large for my machine, an eraser and a brush to clean the keys. With them was a short note: 'Let me know if there is anything else you need, won't you? I'm not making you nervous, am I? I do hope I'm not making you nervous. My prayers and affection are with you and for you. L.'

This was the only sign he made of impatience, though the opening of his management at the St James's hung on the delivery of the script. When at last he got it, not long, I'm afraid, before rehearsals were due to start, he invited my wife and me across to Notley Abbey. When we got there he came out to open the car door, and said: 'What sort of nose do you think the Duke has?' He was beginning, as his way is, to build the character from its physical appearance.

During the run of the play, if, as very occasionally happened, he tripped over a line and produced a spoonerism, I would receive a little note, such as: 'Tonight I said' . . . so-and-so. . . . 'I'm *damn* sorry. I can't say more.' And when he was directing the play in New York, even though he was at the same time playing in *Antony and Cleopatra* and *Caesar and Cleopatra*, he would somehow manage to write immensely long letters keeping me in touch with everything that was going on. No writer could ask for more sympathetic treatment than that.

Sir Terence Rattigan

He has been in only one of my plays, and then I was reluctant to have him. 'Reluctant to have Olivier?' I can hear the cry of outrage. 'In one of *his* plays. He must be mad or joking!' I'm not joking, but I may very well have been mad; but please consider the circumstances.

On 1 January 1953 I woke up with the customary blinding hangover and, later in the day, to the equally blinding thought that this was Coronation Year and I ought to do something about it. Many things, I knew, were being written, composed and choreographed for the occasion, and all the talented people who were writing, composing or choreographing such things had had certainly many months start of me. If I was to get a play written, cast, rehearsed and opened in London by June I would have to work fast. Very fast indeed if you bear in mind that on that grim New Year's morning I didn't even have a play to write. Not a glimmer. Not a notion. Blank.

By the middle of February the blank was about halfway to becoming *The Sleeping Prince*, which I had already decided was to be billed as an 'Occasional Fairy-Tale'. So as not to compete in any way with the other doubtless more important and certainly more portentous *oeuvres d'occasion* that were being readied all over the land, I had decided, by deliberate intent, to revert to a style of very light comedy with which I had begun my career but which, seventeen years later, I was supposed to have outgrown. I had indeed supposed so myself; but this was a very special 'occasion'.

The idea, conceived in a rush (as perhaps all light comedies should be), was based on the familiar comedic formula of standing a well-worn dramatic (in this case, romantic) cliché on its head, and enjoying the results. In *French Without Tears* a *femme fatale*, far from destroying a relationship between two great friends, actually makes a friendship between two deadly enemies. In *The Sleeping Prince* the Regent of Carpathia (a name carefully chosen for its echoes of Anthony Hope and Strauss operettas), far from being the irresistibly attractive *Königliche Höheit* who longs to escape the bondage of royal duty for the bliss of anonymity and the joys of ordinary love, is, in fact, a quite unattractive, very conscientious, extremely mundane little man who is dedicated to the routine of his job, which happens to be that of acting head of state, but, apart from the accident of birth, could equally well have been that of stationmaster at King's Cross; and as for 'the joys of ordinary love', he finds them agreeable enough, provided that in no circumstances whatever may they interrupt his rigorous routine, nor endure at the outside, longer than an hour. Besides, in his world of strict royal punctilio, which he has never questioned nor found irksome, such 'loves' – and there have been myriads of them – can never be 'ordinary' – at least not for his partner, for he is the kind of prince who will expect to be called 'Royal Highness' even in bed. 'Prince Uncharming', in fact, and I venture to think rather closer to the truth of pre-First World War royalty than the romantic legend.

For I had set the play in 1911, at the time when 'royals' and high personages from all over the world were gathering in London for the coronation of King George V and Queen Mary, much as they would be doing in June 1953 when I had planned for my 'occasional fairy-tale' to open. The plot was frail practically to the point of invisibility. The busy Prince can find only one brief hour in his four-day visit for the perfunctory practice of his favourite sport. A chorus girl is hastily acquired as partner but she proves, to the prince's intense dismay, to prefer the romantic cliché to the unromantic reality. If she is going to be seduced at all, it must be to the accompaniment of *tzigane* music, quotations from *Antony and Cleopatra*, and dialogue about her eyes being like 'twin pools' and her hair being like 'spun gold', about the burdens of royalty and the Prince's need for the 'ennobling love of a pure young woman' to help him carry them – such dialogue, in fact, as she feels is proper to a royal seduction. There is no time for the Prince to get another girl, and this girl has at least the merit of being there, on the couch, pleasantly bemused by vodka and plainly ready, if the Prince will only say the words, to comply. Hating himself, he provides the *tzigane* music and says all the expected words; but then, to his horror and anguish, he finds that she has taken them seriously, and has decided to stay with him not for an hour but for life. His frenzied attempts to disentangle himself from this imbroglio thereafter make the whole play, together with his genuine transformation from Prince Un-charming, if not into Prince Charming, at least into Prince Half-Way-Human.

No slighter a plot than *French Without Tears*, perhaps, but certainly hardly more substantial. But I didn't *want* it to be a *French Without Tears*. I knew I'd get hell from the critics if they thought I'd seriously meant this airy trifle to be the next step, after *The Deep Blue Sea*, in my development as a drama-tist. No, I meant it purely as a little nonsense for a great occasion. A non-star cast, a light production and a limited run. Those were my ideas on the night when the telephone went in my study at Sunningdale and I lifted the receiver to hear the distinctive, dulcet-harsh tones of the most famous voice, after Winston Churchill's, in the Anglo-Saxon world.

I knew its owner well, but not so well as to suppose that a call after midnight was going to be about the weather. Some-thing was afoot, I thought, and afoot something most certainly was.

After only the minimal exchange of 'darling old boys' and 'loveys' the voice changed into that quietly imperious register: 'I hear you're writing a play for the coronation that might suit Vivien and me.'

There seemed only one answer to this and I gave it.

'No.'

'You mean you're not writing a play for the coronation?'

'I mean I'm not writing a play that would suit you and Vivien.'

Bold stuff, you'll agree. It would have been even bolder if

I hadn't consented, at the end of about half an hour, to 'let him have a glance at it, old ducky, when it was finished, so that he could judge all that for himself'. And he rang off.

I had given him with as much eloquence as one can muster at such an hour, in duologue with such a voice, all the deeply compelling reasons why I thought such casting would be utterly fatal, both for the Oliviers and for me. My little 'occasional fairy-tale' couldn't contain one of those two gigantic talents, let alone both. And how on earth could Larry persuade an audience that he was 'Prince Uncharming' when he had made even Richard III into one of the most sexually attractive characters ever to disgrace a stage? And how on earth could darling Vivien, one of nature's grand-duchesses if ever I saw one, walk on to a stage as a chorus girl thrilled to her Brooklynese death at the prospect of meeting a real grand duke in the flesh? And what would the critics say about it all? Oh no, it just wasn't on.

But it was. And, I suppose, from the moment I heard that voice on the telephone that night I knew it was going to be. He is accustomed to getting what he wants, and what he wanted, for reasons that were then mysterious to me, was *The Sleeping Prince*.

So the news was trumpeted abroad to an over-expectant public that Laurence Olivier and Vivien Leigh would appear together in a new play, written specially for them by Terence Rattigan, to honour the occasion of the coronation of Her Majesty, Queen Elizabeth II. Disaster and humiliation stared us, I really and sincerely believed, in the face. We could quite easily end up in the Tower.

Things looked even worse when, just as we were about to rehearse, Vivien went down with a serious illness and we were obliged to postpone production until the autumn. My 'occasional' nonsense, for which the 'occasion' was now past and gone, and which, by November, had almost been forgotten, was now billed as a Laurence Olivier Production–H. M. Tennent Ltd major dramatic attraction for the new London theatrical season. The press of the world were now announcing its advent almost daily, the already over-expectant public had got themselves into such a frenzy of excitement that they had bought out the entire Manchester Opera House solid at double prices for our pre-London week within hours of seats going on sale, and the queues for the Phoenix stretched out of sight. It seemed now as if we wouldn't even get as far as the Tower. How could we escape being lynched in Cambridge Circus? Only by magic.

The magic happened: Larry's performance. (Not, unhappily, Vivien's, because my original prediction proved, alas, only too accurate. She was, as she and I – and perhaps Larry – always knew, miscast. She made a marvellously gallant try at being a Brooklyn chorus girl, and devoted to the task all the brilliance of her exquisite technique in comedy, but she could never overcome the handicap of that innate grand-ducality of which I have spoken). But, Larry, as my Prince, was – well – magic.

What makes magic is genius, and what makes genius, we are assured, is the infinite capacity for taking pains, and if that definition be correct, Larry has it in abundance. The demands of 'total acting' are indeed total. I would watch in rehearsal utterly spellbound as, over the weeks, he built his performance slowly and with immense application from a mass of tiny details, some discarded, some retained. 'Are you going to say it like that, Larry?' Vivien would ask. 'I don't know yet,' Larry would reply: 'Let's go on.' Vivien, by contrast, always knew exactly how she was going to say anything, and Larry's continuous experimenting would bother her, as it must, I suppose, any actress playing with him who relies, as did Vivien, on an exact and assured technique. Sometimes he would break her up into helpless giggles. 'Is it as funny as that?' he would ask anxiously. Vivien, unable to reply, would nod, wiping her eyes. 'Terry, what do you think?' In paroxysms of laughter myself, I would say: 'Yes, marvellous.' Then he might consider, frowning: 'No, I think it's too much. It's out.' And out it would be for no discernible reason except that we had both laughed too much and *we* weren't the audience. His instinct for such things is superb, and he was almost certainly right.

But many, many things were *in*, and gloriously in. From a host of marvellously conceived little inventions, all perfectly characteristic of my prosaic Prince, I can select only two. The Prince prided himself on what he considered his extreme fluency in English slang, using phrases like 'cheerioh' and 'old hat' as if – so I think went my stage direction – he'd just coined them. Larry seized on that eagerly (indeed he was extraordinarily faithful to my stage directions : most directors don't even read them) and added his own embroidery – an Oxford accent so extreme that it contorted every vowel into a strangled cry of pain. 'Cheerioh' became 'chirieuh', 'old hat' became 'euold het'. And a complacent smirk would spread over the Prince's usually unsmiling features in pleasure at having hit not only on the correct English idiom but also the correct 'Oxford' pronunciation. Irresistible, and perfectly in order. So *would* the Prince have learned his English slang.

And then another still tiny but perhaps even more revealing point. At a certain moment in the seduction scene, when the Prince is having perforce to use the kind of dialogue that his seducee wants to hear, he is rambling on about his need for 'true love', and his difficulty in finding it, while giving an occasional impatient glance at the clock. The line reads : ' Ah yes, my child, here I am, having reached the age of fort – thirty-nine, and I have never found etc etc.' This was, I think, the only line in the whole play that Larry asked me to change. He wanted to say : ' Here I am, having reached the age of forty – ' and then stop short of adding the three or four extra years that were the probable truth. I agreed, but frankly didn't see how he could get the laugh, since the audience might well take forty as correct. He assured me he would. He did – and one of the biggest laughs in the play. It was done by a split-second's freeze of alarm, the tiniest of tiny pauses, and the continuation of the rest of the speech on the slightly hysterical note of 'danger overcome'.

I have said ' more revealing ' because, where fort – thirty-nine ' was fairly sure-fire but rather unsubtle, Larry's ' forty ' showed him to have mastered perfectly the arts of the true light comedian, and such arts I hadn't expected him to possess. That sounds impertinent, and it is, but to get laughs as Justice Shallow chasing an imaginary bee round the stage is one thing, to get them on a disyllable by exactness of timing and inflexion is another. Ask Noël Coward. Ask Rex Harrison. They are the present two great masters of the craft, and they both know how appallingly difficult it is. I think they get many of their effects by pure instinct. Larry got his by his usual methods of total study, total acting and, at length, total reward.

Where I had expected my flimsy little confection to be burst asunder by the vastness of his talent, it was in fact held firmly in shape by his quietly magisterial performance, which, while remaining resolutely faithful to his author's frivolous intentions, succeeded in adding to the part those dimensions that one looks for from great acting; and where I had feared that my 'Prince Uncharming' would inevitably become, in his hands, 'Prince Utterly Irresistible', those fears were for ever laid to rest when, at the dress rehearsal, I went into his dressing room just before curtain to be confronted by a rather dull-looking little man, with an anaemic complexion, a thin, prissy, humourless mouth, hair parted in the middle and plastered repulsively downwards over his ears, and a sad-looking monocle glued over his right eye. It was only when I saw that he was dressed in Edwardian evening dress, with an Order round his neck, that I recognized, and embraced, my own, true, living, breathing, Sleeping Prince.

We were saved from the Tower. And I have loved the man this side of idolatry, ever since – and frankly, not always 'this side'.

Bernard Braden

One night in February 1949 I attended the five-hundredth performance of *A Streetcar named Desire* in New York. What impressed me most was the performance of Marlon Brando in the role of Stanley. The following morning I sailed for London to try and make a living as an actor; several months later I heard that auditions were being held by H. M. Tennent for the London production of *Streetcar* and found that the impact of Brando had been so strong that I could do a well-nigh perfect impersonation of him, and even remembered some of the speeches verbatim.

Accordingly, and with total confidence, I turned up for auditions at the Globe Theatre, only to find that all the actors assembled there were auditioning for the lesser part of Mitch. We were all asked to take off our jackets and roll up our sleeves and join the queue in the wings. As I got closer to the head of the queue I realized that the girl who was reading opposite the auditionees was an actress I'd met the previous week at a party, so when my turn came I walked on to the stage and asked her, *sotto voce*, to turn to a certain scene. Before anyone could stop us we had launched into one of Stanley's main exchanges with Blanche, with me doing my perfect impression of Brando. This was allowed to continue for some time before a voice from the stalls said: 'This is all very interesting, but it's the wrong part.'

I recognized the voice from films, and it was the first time I realized that Sir Laurence Olivier was involved in the production. In fact, he was directing it. I mumbled a palpable lie, that we'd inadvertently started on the wrong page, and the voice said: 'Would you *deign* to read the part of Mitch?'

I deigned, attempting my impeccable impersonation of Karl Malden, who'd played the part of Mitch in the Broadway production. I was told I might be called for another audition, but before I left the voice proceeded from the darkness of the stalls into the reflected light of the pit, and Sir Laurence Olivier said quietly. 'Do you strip all right?' I said I did and went happily away in the sure knowledge that he'd been impressed by my Brando imitation, since only Stanley was required to bare his chest in the play.

A week later my agent called to say I was required for another audition. 'Stanley?' 'Mitch.'

This time there were other voices in the stalls, and I gave a fairly lethargic reading of the part of Mitch. Then Sir Laurence said: 'Would you mind reading us the Napoleonic Code scene of Stanley's?' Enthusiastically I went into my impression of Brando. This was followed by a whispered argument in the darkened stalls, only part of which I could hear. Somebody said: 'But nobody's ever heard of him', and then I heard the voice of Sir Laurence Olivier say: 'I don't care who he is, he's an actor.'

I rate it as one of the two or three compliments I really treasure.

About two months later we went into rehearsal for *A Streetcar named Desire*, with me in the role of Mitch.

In the meantime I'd had a cartilage removed from my left knee and was still walking with a cane. Since Mitch was involved in a good deal of physical action during the play there was a strong possibility that the first day of rehearsal would be my last. I left the cane at the stage door and somehow managed the flight of stairs down to the rehearsal area. It was Sir Laurence who noticed the blood on my left sock, so there was no point in not confessing to the operation. Instead of firing me he gave me a number of exercises that would strengthen the leg, and reworked a lot of stage business so that I wouldn't have to put weight on that leg. It was some time later that I learned he'd undergone a similar operation while playing Richard III, a role requiring more strenuous activity than that of Mitch, and had continued with his performances.

Great actors are supposed to take themselves rather seriously, but Sir Laurence showed his sense of humour early on in rehearsal. The first week we sat in a semicircle, simply reading the play. Sir Laurence sat facing us, but flanked on either side by four or five people whose duties seemed to consist of passing messages to him from the wings. One morning an envelope appeared from the wings and was passed from hand to hand until it reached Sir Laurence, by which time we had stopped reading. There was silence while he studied the envelope for some time. Then he said aloud: 'Laurence Olivier c/o the *Sunday Graphic*. . . . Oh well, they know they can always get me there.'

I had done some stage work in Canada, even to the point of directing plays, but Sir Laurence added a new concept to my idea of theatre production. One morning I was sitting idly in the stalls watching him direct Bonar Colleano and Renée Asherson in a scene that involved a good deal of flurried movement. Eventually he went on the stage to illustrate what he wanted them to do. It seemed incredibly simple as he did it, but somehow they couldn't reproduce it. I thought them very stupid. That same day I was rehearsing a scene with Vivien Leigh in which I was required to lift her from the floor, turn her round to a wall and lift the shade off a lamp so that Blanche could be seen in a bare light. Finally he came on stage to show me how to do it. He did it three times in quick succession, and it was like watching quicksilver. I could no more have reproduced it than fly, but I realized that to anyone sitting in the stalls it would have looked incredibly simple. I achieved a semblance of it eventually, but it was never in a class with what he did.

After the play opened he called few rehearsals. His method seemed to be to give a concise note that conveyed everything that was required. There was one elaborate fight scene in *Streetcar* that involved all the men in the cast and had been worked out in rehearsal to give the maximum effect of reality. It depended on split-second timing from everyone involved, and there was one moment that usually drew a gasp from the audience because they assumed that someone had accidentally been knocked unconscious. This continued for about two weeks, then we began to miss the gasp, but we didn't know why. One night Sir Laurence came round and assembled everyone involved. He said: ' I was watching the play tonight, and after the knockabout scene a man behind me turned to his companion and said: " Not a very good fight ".' That's *all* he said. The next night the gasp was back again.

All this was more than twenty years ago, and for me there are still two Laurence Oliviers. One is the man who gave me my first chance in the London theatre, and by treating me as a professional made me behave as a professional; a man who encouraged me to call him ' Larry ' and still does on the rare occasions when we meet. The other is the well-known actor of stage and screen whose work I admired before I came to London, and still do. He is Sir Laurence Olivier.

Sir John Clements

LOGAN GOURLAY: You are a contemporary of Olivier's and you have been working in the theatre and in films for about the same number of years, but as far as I know you have never acted together.

JOHN CLEMENTS: That's true, unfortunately – for me anyway. As young actors we were both under contract to Korda but we never appeared together in the same film. I knew him only slightly then but over the years we became friends, though we never worked together.

LG: How did it come about that you took over from him as director of the Chichester Theatre in 1966?

JC: It all started in Brighton really. I've lived there for years, and on one occasion after his marriage to Vivien Leigh was over and he was looking for a place to live outside London I invited him to take over our house because we were going away for a bit. Well, he liked Brighton so much he bought a house nearby and we became neighbours. One weekend he asked me in for a drink and over the gins and tonic he told me that he wanted to be free to concentrate on the National, and out of the blue he said: 'How would you like to take over Chichester?' I was surprised to say the least, but looking back now I'm delighted he asked me.

LG: Did he interfere in any way when you took over at first?

JC: Not at all. He left me to get on with it. He was fully occupied himself with the National, but even if he'd had the time he's not the kind of man who would have interfered after he'd made his decision.

LG: As you know, some of his critics have said that his policy of running the National as an actor-manager was wrong and that he should have devoted himself entirely to acting, because it's impossible for any man – even Olivier – to play demanding roles and at the same time cope with the problems of running a theatre.

JC: I'm not of course putting myself on the same level as Larry, but speaking as someone who has been an actor-manager for many years I should like to say that whatever I've done as an actor – however good, bad or indifferent any of my performances have been – I honestly do not believe that they would have been any better if I had not been the manager as well. I have the kind of mind that can, as it were, departmentalize itself – and so has Larry, obviously. Without it no one should try to be an actor-manager, but with it the job is possible.

I believe that the criticisms of him as actor-manager at the National are valid on one count only, and that is quantity, not quality. If it's claimed that he might have given us more performances if he hadn't had to manage the theatre as well, then I say perhaps. But that is the only criticism that can be levelled.

LG: Isn't it a serious criticism, however, that because of his managerial responsibilities the public were deprived of the opportunities of seeing him in some of the great roles?

JC: God almighty, there aren't many that he hasn't already played.

LG: It has also been said that the cares of management must have used up and dissipated some of the creative energy that might have been given to his acting.

JC: If you take his performance in *The Dance of Death* as a fairly recent example I'd like to say that he couldn't have given a better performance if he had been wrapped in cottonwool for three years instead of running the National. This of course is the mark of a great man – that he has the ability and the energy to give that kind of performance and still run the theatre and cope with all the problems. God knows, there are lots of problems.

LG: As an actor-manager yourself running Chichester have you never felt you would like to be free of all the problems and responsibilities so that you could concentrate entirely on acting?

JC: Frankly, no. If I were at Chichester as just a member of the company I suppose I'd probably play more parts. Quantity again, not quality. But then there's the other side of the question – and I hope this doesn't sound arrogant – but if I weren't running the theatre myself I might find myself in the hands of a manager who did things that perhaps I wouldn't do that would irritate me very much and get between me and my performance. Of course, what I do myself may be awful, but at least I believe in it and I'm not upset by somebody else interfering and doing what I consider wrong. I don't mean somebody else is bound to be wrong. What I mean is that if I disagree with somebody else's conception and ideas I can be frustrated to such an extent that a good performance is impossible.

LG: It has often been said about actor-managers that they tend to take the best parts for themselves and that they don't give the fullest opportunities to the other members of the company.

JC: If anyone claims that Larry Olivier has ever grabbed the best parts for himself regardless of other actors they don't know anything about the man or his career. He's generous, perhaps to a fault, with his fellow-players.

LG: His critics say that the emphasis at the National has been mainly on Olivier as the star actor.

JC: They forget that he chose an opening production for the National in which he didn't appear – *Hamlet* with Peter O'Toole. Over the years he has built up a strong company with actors like Robert Stephens and he has invited other star actors to appear, like John Gielgud, Paul Scofield and Albert Finney. It's nonsense to suggest that he's run it for the glorification of himself. At the same time, however, if he hadn't tackled some of the big parts like Othello and Shylock he'd have been criticized for shirking his responsibilities as an actor.

LG: Of all his performances, which do you think have been the most memorable and impressive?

JC: Without hesitation I'd put his Captain in *The Dance of Death* at the top of the list. It was a staggeringly brilliant performance. Of course he's given many other brilliant performances; in fact he can hardly fail to do anything else.

I've never seen so complete an actor in my life. He has complete control over his voice, his movements – everything physical that goes into a performance. He knows exactly what he wants to do and whether one agrees with him or not, he does it to perfection within his own conception. When he played Othello as a Negro he was a Negro in every muscle and sinew. As Shylock at the National he was a Jew in every fibre of his being. As Richard III – which was incidentally one of the most memorable performances of his whole career – you felt that the physical defects were congenital, not assumed. Then in *Henry IV, Part One*, when he played Hotspur, he was virility personified. The following night when he played Shallow in *Part Two* you felt that this frail, white-haired little man would be blown across stage like a leaf in the autumn wind. You simply could not believe that it was the same actor who had played Hotspur the previous night.

Physical control – complete physical command – is the explanation. I remember one day about a month before he started to rehearse for *Othello* he said to me: 'You've got a much deeper voice than I have. That's what's needed for Othello.' I went to the first night and out of him, with no effort, no strain, came a voice that was two octaves lower than mine. It seemed effortless, but of course behind it there must have been hours and hours of work and concentration. He has an infinite capacity for taking pains.

LG: In the early years I believe he was very concerned about what he thought were physical shortcomings. He thought his hair line was too low, for example, and he used to shave it back. And he used to wear elevators to add to his height.

JC: As I said, I didn't know him well in the early years, but I remember he was very handsome and dashing and I shouldn't have thought he needed any artificial aids to improve his appearance. But then one did all kinds of absurd things as a young actor. I remember I used to have my ears stuck back with fish skin because I thought they stuck out too much. One grows out of that kind of nonsense.

LG: Have you ever seen Olivier in a performance that disappointed you in any way?

JC: No, he's never disappointed me. Whatever he does he is always stimulating and interesting. I've disagreed sometimes with his conception of a part – Othello as a Negro, for example. But within that conception he gave an exciting performance.

LG: It has been said that he has excelled more in comedy than in tragedy. Do you agree?

JC: It's too simplified a comparison. I don't think it can be made at his level of skill and achievement. He has the most amazing ability – instinct, if you like – to find the comedy that most actors would miss in any heavy or tragic part he plays. He did it for example in *The Dance of Death*, which he made frightfully funny at times. He also did it in *Richard* III and even in *Lear*. But I don't think for a moment that's the same thing as saying he's more of a comic actor than a tragedian. He's both.

I've got a print on the wall somewhere that sums it all up. It shows the masks of comedy and tragedy – the two muses – pulling Garrick both ways, and the caption says: 'Don't either of you think you can claim him. He belongs to both of you.' Or words to that effect.

I think that applies to Larry Olivier too. He will go down to posterity, like Garrick, as one of the greatest actors of the English stage.

John Osborne

LOGAN GOURLAY: In your early career as an actor before *Look Back in Anger* made you a famous playwright, did you have any contact with Olivier?

JOHN OSBORNE: None. My first meeting with him was after *Look Back in Anger* had opened at the Royal Court. He had seen it and said that in his opinion it was a piece of shit. But somebody whose opinion he respected, met him one evening and told him that he was absolutely wrong about the play and that he must see it again. So they got into a taxi and went to the theatre. They had no trouble buying a couple of tickets at the box office and they went to their seats. It was in the days when the Court was doing rep., and when the curtain went up it was a play called *Cards of Identity*, which I happened to be in as an actor. Olivier came round to see me afterwards and offered me a part in the film of *Macbeth*, which he was planning to make at that time. I remember he said, 'You're like me. You like putting on make-up.' He was right about that.

LG: So he liked you as an actor, but had he changed his mind about your play?

JO: I've never been sure. But I think he decided at that time that George Devine was doing something at the Court that couldn't be overlooked. I imagine he said to himself: 'Ah, old George has got something going on here that could be interesting – something up-to-date that I can't ignore.' Like a lot of complicated people Olivier can also be very simple. He can decide that there's a simple short cut to some kind of contemporary truth or attitude that he should adopt. All he's got to do

is step round the corner. Anyway, he decided there was something new he wanted – or needed in his career – round the
corner in Sloane Square at the Court. Later on in his life I think
he first became interested for similar reasons in Joan Plowright.
I mean as an actress. (His reasons for marrying her are his own
affair and they're none of my business.) But I remember George
Devine and Tony Richardson thought she represented the new
kind of actress – she had reality and truth as opposed to the
old Shaftesbury Avenue glitter. I didn't agree, but Olivier was
obviously influenced by their opinion.

LG: When you wrote *The Entertainer* did you have him in
mind?

JO: Not at all. I know that he himself thought I'd written it for
him but he was deluding himself. I've never written anything
for any actor ever because it's an impractical thing to do. And
apart from anything else it gets in between you and what
you're trying to create. If you see it in terms of some actor's
face or voice, it's hopeless. What happened was that when I
was writing the play Olivier did in fact ring George Devine and
ask if I were doing a new play that might interest him. George,
knowing my attitude, then rang me very tentatively and said,
'Do you think there's a part for Laurence?' Incidentally his
own generation – people like John Gielgud and Ralph
Richardson – all call him Laurence. It's the younger ones who
seem to call him Larry. Anyway at that time he and Vivien
Leigh were very much the theatrical royal couple. They played
the roles to the hilt and they obviously enjoyed it all. So when
George asked me if there would be a part for the 'King' I was
stunned. All I could reply at first was: 'I don't know and don't
ask me till I've finished.'

LG: When was it decided that the 'King' would play Archie
Rice in *The Entertainer*?

JO: Not for a little while. After he had read the first two acts
he thought he wanted to play the father, for the obvious reason
that it seemed to be the best part in the play. Then of course
he changed his mind when he'd read the whole play. At one

stage Vivien wanted to appear in it, too, playing the part of the wife. They were very keen to play in it together.

LG: Why didn't they?

JO: Well, he kept saying: 'The trouble is that Vivien is too beautiful to play this kind of part.' And a great deal of fruitless discussion went on. There was one conversation I'll never forget. It took place in the Connaught Hotel, where they happened to be staying at the time, and they sat around having a serious discussion about whether or not she should wear a rubber mask to make her look plain and ugly. I thought it was a ludicrous suggestion and I still do. However, although she didn't play the part – with or without a rubber mask – she made her influence felt during rehearsals almost as though she were a leading member of the cast. There was a great deal of backbiting and niggling and I'm afraid there were quite a few rows. There was a superb one I remember between George and Vivien.

LG: Do you think she was afraid he had made the wrong decision when he said he would appear in the play?

JO: I don't think so. She was mainly concerned about how he would do it. But there's no doubt about the fact that almost all of his friends thought he was making a terrible mistake, and they never stopped telling him. I must say that I formed the opinion that most of his friends at that time were very stupid people. They were frankly little more than third-rate sycophants. They had nothing to say really except that he was marvellous and the play was bloody awful. By their standards they may well have been right. But their comments were anything but helpful to the production. In fact they were quite destructive.

LG: Was there ever any possibility of it being cancelled before the opening?

JO: No, never. He was committed to doing it and that was that. However, his reasons for doing it were mixed. One of them, as I've indicated, was that he wanted to keep up with the contemporary bandwagon. Still, it should be remembered it was a daring and courageous thing for him to do then. Nowadays they all do it – Richardson and Gielgud go to the Court for £50 a week, but they hadn't then. So Olivier was leading the way. And one mustn't be unfair about it. After all he was the Establishment actor and he was doing a non-Establishment play by a non-Establishment writer. Naturally his Establishment sycophants were prophesying doom and disaster. It couldn't have been easy for him. Especially when you remember that in his complex way he's a self-conscious man, very aware of his role in the history of the twentieth century and his place in the English hierarchy. Up to a point, I think, his attitude is that he is making history, particularly English history, apart from just appearing in historical plays. But this is just my interpretation. I don't claim to know him deeply. I don't think many people do. He's a very elusive character. Still, from what I do know of him there's one side of him that's rather grand – solidly English and conservative.

LG: Do you think his titles have been important to him?

JO: I don't think he's a simple title-hunting snob. But I think he likes being a member of the English Establishment and he thinks he should be. I suppose this attitude developed rather early on during the war, for example, when he wasn't merely an actor playing parts, he was contributing to the war effort. He wasn't just making *Henry V* as an exercise in putting Shakespeare on the screen, he was helping to boost morale and that kind of thing. The authorities put him in a rather special position, whether he wanted it or not. But he probably reacted to it well because, going further back, he had a high-church Anglican upbringing which gave him a sense of ritual and responsibility, and of course he's always had an innate theatrical sense. So it wouldn't be difficult for him to accept – and play – the role of the rather grand Establishment actor.

LG: Were you worried at the time of *The Entertainer* that his fame and prominence would swamp your play?

JO: Yes, I was, up to a point. And there's no doubt in my view that he did throw it out of balance. The production did suffer in a way, not because of his performance, which was brilliant, but because of the attitude and interpretation of the public, who regarded it as a vehicle for Olivier. The emphasis was too much on him and the other people in the cast, particularly Brenda de Banzie and George Relph, who were outstandingly good, were somewhat overlooked.

LG: Were you pleased with the film version of *The Entertainer*?

JO: It was very difficult to set up in the first place. The budget was fairly high – about £200,000 – for what was clearly a very doubtful commercial prospect. It was made mostly on location at Morecambe and it was very exacting for Olivier, who was appearing in *Coriolanus* at Stratford at the same time. He hired an ambulance so that he could lie down and sleep as he was being driven after the performance from Stratford to Morecambe. The trouble about filming *The Entertainer* was that it was such a theatrical piece that it was almost impossible to transfer it to another medium. Still, he succeeded as well as anyone could, though he knew he could never be as effective as he'd been on the stage. Oddly enough, what I thought was his best stage performance in the part was never seen by the public. It was at one of the dress rehearsals on a Saturday afternoon. The doors were open and the noise of the traffic was coming in, but what was happening on stage was so good that everything else was forgotten. Of course, he may have been as good in other performances that I didn't see. One that I did see, and will always remember, was the last night in New York, when the audience – which is usually undemonstrative over there – stood up and cheered. The manager said he'd never seen it happen before. The first night there was memorable, too, for a sad reason. George Kaufman, the American writer, died right in the middle of the second act right in the middle of the stalls and had to be carried out.

LG: Many people thought that Olivier with his background would not fully understand the part of a third-rate, seedy music-hall comic like Archie Rice, and they were surprised he was so good in the part. Were you?

JO: I knew he was a great comic actor and his range would extend to a part like that. I think a certain self-dislike exists in him alongside that feeling about being a grand and important figure in history. Once again I'm speculating because one can never be certain about other people's characters, but I suspect that Olivier has a feeling sometimes that he is a deeply hollow man. That doesn't mean that he *is* a hollow man, but he knows what it's like to feel hollow. And that's why – or it's one of the reasons – he was so good as Archie Rice. Olivier understands that kind of character and his feelings of inadequacy – of being fifth-rate. All comics are ready to duck even when they appear to be aggressively confident, perhaps even more so then. Olivier knows the ready-to-duck mentality.

LG: You have written a newspaper article attacking him and the way he has run the National Theatre. Do you still have the same views?

JO: Yes, I do. When I wrote the article people said I was having one of my periodic bouts of madness and I was attacked in turn. Generally I'm not in favour of public slanging matches. I prefer not to say anything when I'm asked for my opinion of other writers, for example, because I don't think one should criticize someone else who's trying to do something as frightfully difficult as creative work. But I suddenly thought somebody, in the interests of the theatre generally, had to break the conspiracy of silence about the National. A great many people in the profession think it's bloody awful but they don't say so publicly because they don't want to hurt people's feelings or because they don't want to rock the boat. Well, I finally decided to speak up.

LG: What are your main criticisms of the National and of Olivier as the man in charge?

JO: Since it began nearly ten years ago with Peter O'Toole's *Hamlet* it has, I think, combined the worst aspects of the commercial theatre with those of an institution – a stuffy institution. I also think Olivier is the least suitable person to run a national theatre. He always wanted to be an actor-manager, but that is something quite different from being the administrator of a theatrical institution. He's got the wrong kind of temperament for a job like that. On the one hand he wants to be trendy, or to keep up with public taste, or get beyond it; and on the other he is also, I think, publicly very orthodox and conservative. These conflicting attitudes are disastrous if you are running a theatre like the National. Another defect is that, I suspect, he can succumb to envy – most actors do at one time or another – envy of other people's successes.

LG: Can you name anyone who would be ideally equipped for the job of running the National?

JO: The ideal would be someone like the great Diaghilev. Someone who is absolutely single-minded, entirely egotistical, who takes no notice of what anyone else is doing or thinking. Someone who concentrates completely on his own plans. He is setting the styles and trends and fashions, not following. He doesn't really care what the public thinks or what's happening at the box office (though it can't be ignored, I suppose). It's a certain kind of artistic temperament and hardly anyone ever has it. It's ridiculous – and unfair – to expect someone who's a great actor like Olivier to have this kind of temperament – to be a Diaghilev. Even if you do have it it's difficult to sustain your influence. Diaghilev's particular period, with its peculiar combination of artists, composers and dancers that affected the other arts and public life, sustained itself for only a relatively short time.

LG: Do you know of anyone at the moment with this kind of Diaghilev temperament?

JO: George Devine had it to an extent, I think, and used it successfully at the Court, but it virtually killed him. The pressures are enormous and the responsibilities crushing. And remember he didn't do any acting. Yet here we have Olivier playing thumping great roles like Othello, which apart from anything else require the physical stamina of a long-distance truck driver, and at the same time trying to run a theatre – not just an ordinary theatre but a national enterprise, more or less a nationalized industry. It's impossible. And to make matters worse there's the disastrous influence of Kenneth Tynan. Whatever his qualities as a writer and critic he has, I think, absolutely the wrong attitude to running a theatre. It's a sort of intellectual spivery that Olivier mistakes for up-to-date awareness and flair. He's so afraid of being thought old-hat that he's allowed himself to be sadly misguided by Tynan. At least, thank God, he hasn't allowed Tynan to talk him into a nude *Macbeth* with 'bunny' witches.

LG: Were you closely involved with the National when they presented *A Bond Honoured*?

JO: Yes, fairly. Of course it wasn't my own play. It was an adaptation from the Spanish of Lope de Vega, and it wasn't a great success, which may have been as much my fault as theirs. Anyway, I found the whole atmosphere of the place was stuffy and institutional. All very gloomy. No spark. Everyone seemed to be afraid to expand. You didn't get the impression that talents – old or new – were being developed or liberated in the right way. People were too afraid of doing the wrong thing. They were behaving like civil servants, not like people of the theatre.

LG: Did you like anything about it?

JO: Yes, they have one good rule there. No one outside the company is allowed to go round backstage and worry the cast before a first night. I was reminded of it recently because oddly enough Olivier didn't apply it when he went to see a preview of my play *West of Suez*. He went backstage afterwards and he wasn't exactly encouraging in his comments to people in the cast like Ralph Richardson. Now Ralph is a tough, experienced old bird, and he wasn't affected very much. But I know that Olivier has done this on several occasions during the past six or seven years and it can be very destructive. Even if he doesn't say anything, think of the effect, particularly on young and inexperienced actors, if the great Olivier comes round after the performance with a long face. It's demoralizing to say the least, as he must know, and after all he doesn't allow it in his own theatre. It's an example of how insensitive a sensitive actor can sometimes be. Another example of how complex and complicated a highly talented man like Olivier can be.

LG: The word genius has been applied to him as an actor. Would you apply it?

JO: Yes, he is a sort of genius in the sense that he has a peculiar projected imagination as an actor. He can get away with almost anything. He can even get away with being terribly vulgar. I thought, for example, he was unspeakably vulgar as Othello. At the same time he is the only actor who would have had the courage to do something as dreadful as his Othello. His courage is outstanding, though sometimes it's in danger of being wilful obstinacy. I don't think anyone could stop him doing something dreadful like Othello once he had made up his mind, just as I don't think anyone can really direct him. He will ultimately do what he wants to do. He has it all worked out in advance. And curiously enough he sometimes works things out in a simple – but peculiarly arduous – way. I remember when he was preparing to do a play called *Semi-Detached* and I had to go to see him for some reason at his home in Royal Crescent in Brighton. He took me up to his little room – a sort of work room – at the top of the house where he had yards and yards of tape recordings of the Nottingham dialect and accent he had to use in the play. He had obviously spent weeks laboriously perfecting the accent. He had lavished tremendous care on it – literal-minded care – but in the end it didn't really matter. He missed any poetry that might have been there by concentrating too much on the technical aspects. The play was supposed to be a kind of modern Restoration comedy and it was played in a rather naturalistic way. It needed a smaller talent than Olivier's. He sort of swamped it.

LG: Do you think that was an occasion when he was consciously trying to be contemporary?

JO : Yes, I think so, and it didn't come off. He's inclined sometimes not to rely as much on his intuition as he should do. So
he allows himself to be deluded by so-called intellectuals like
Tynan. Like many people who feel that they have been inad-
equately educated, Olivier has an over-reverence for people
who have some kind of academic background. On one occasion
he was talking to me about a director whom he didn't rate very
highly. I happened to say, quite peripherally, that the man had
been to Winchester and Magdalen, and I sensed immediately
that his stock went up with Olivier. He does waver in his judgement of people, and that's another reason why he's not good
as an administrator of a theatre. If you're running the place,
and if you make a decision about someone, you must be consistent about it. You must trust what he is even though you
realize he's not perfect. You must support him completely. It's
the same with a play. Once you have decided to do it, no
matter how difficult it turns out to be, or how much it upsets
some people, you must pursue it from beginning to end. George
Devine was particularly good in this respect. There was never
any pressure, before or after, even if the play was slated in
the papers and the public stayed away in droves. He made you
think it didn't matter and kept up an optimistic atmosphere. It
may sound arrogant but an atmosphere like that is healthy and
productive, as opposed to the atmosphere at the National,
where there is always this feeling of pressure to live up to
institutionalized standards. That in itself is uncreative.

LG : Do you think the National has established any traditions
yet?

JO : No, I'm afraid not. That actor Derek Jocobi who's been
there for several years playing mostly supporting parts, said
the other day – and I thought he was quite funny – that when
he goes abroad and says he's a National Theatre player he might
as well say he's from the National Coal Board. That's an exag-
geration, I suppose, but there's a certain amount of truth in it
because the National hasn't really established itself as a theatre
for the simple reason that it hasn't any clear identity. When
you talk about the National most people think first and fore-

most of Lord Olivier. They may think, too, about Robert Stephens and Maggie Smith, but that's about all. No contemporary writers are associated with it except Peter Nichols, and to a lesser extent Tom Stoppard. They've had a lot of well-known actors there but most of them have been treated rather badly and they've left feeling a bit aggrieved – people like John Gielgud and Irene Worth.

LG : Do you think there's something about the English national character that is inimical to a national theatre?

JO : Probably. Maybe that's why the Court has been such a success. It's such a *shambles* – a typically English pragmatic mess with backstage bitchiness and clash of personalities. Perhaps in the best English sense of the word it's amateur, but it has come up with the goods in an extraordinary consistent way. There have been something like 340 productions, and a lot have been disastrous, admittedly, but more have been excellent. The National of course has had a shorter life but the average level of excellence is lower. Still, in all fairness there have been one or two outstandingly good productions.

LG : Is there any performance of Olivier's at the National or elsewhere that sticks in your mind apart from his Archie Rice in *The Entertainer*?

JO : Sadly I missed many of his definitive Shakespearean performances, like his Richard III. It's a generation gap. When I started going to the theatre I couldn't get a ticket to see him, or I couldn't afford one, or I was working myself as an actor. Recently I thought he was brilliant in Strindberg's *Dance of Death*. Going further back I'm sorry I missed that great double bill when he did Puff in *The Critic* and Oedipus. Very astute that was, to go from the comedy straight into the tragedy. It must have been most effective theatrically, and one can see how it could work technically for an actor who's got sufficient range, as of course he has.

LG : How did you like his film versions of Shakespeare – *Henry V*, *Richard III* and *Hamlet*?

JO: I particularly disliked the Richard. But then I don't know how you can film Shakespeare. I don't think anyone has ever done it really successfully. You can't put Shakespeare on television either. The whole point about Shakespeare in the theatre is that the audience is part of it all. Take the audience away – and the ambience – and it's an entirely different experience. On television it just looks rather ridiculous and rather reduced, as opera and ballet do on television. Then I think that television does reduce, and minimize, most experiences. Olivier has done very little of it, and that's very wise of him. I don't think he's stayed away from it in any sense of being grand. I think he just knows instinctively that it's not for him. And he's right. No actor of any magnitude is ever going to show his magnitude on television. It's full of good, but middle-of-the-road, actors. They give impressive performances on the box but if you stuck them on a stage in a really big taxing part that Olivier can tackle they would be completely lost.

LG: How do you think he should direct his career from now on?

JO: It's none of my business really and it would be presumptuous of me to suggest anything. However I remember he told me once that the thing he wanted to do most of all was to direct films, because he said that gave him the most concentrated power, and he enjoyed doing it more than anything else. I don't know if he really meant it or if he still has the same ambition. However I do think he would be better employed directing films than accepting some of the film parts he's played recently. At this stage of his career there's a great danger of being lured by those guest celebrity cameo parts. I know everyone raved about *Oh, What A Lovely War* but I thought it was extremely bad and he should never have been in it. In general theatrical terms I think he should give up trying to run the National Theatre. He should let someone else do it – anyone except Tynan – and concentrate entirely on being an actor. He's a great one.

Tony Richardson

LOGAN GOURLAY: Directing Laurence Olivier in *The Entertainer* must have been a large undertaking for a young director. Were you over-awed when you first heard you were going to do it?

TONY RICHARDSON: I was terrified. It was the first time I had directed a big star; but I needn't have worried. Larry couldn't have been more helpful and generous to me. I just had to make a suggestion and he responded immediately. From my point of view as a young inexperienced director he was a joy to work with.

It turned out to be quite a long association, because we did *The Entertainer* three times. First at the Royal Court, then at the Palace when it transferred to the West End and later on Broadway. And after that I directed him in the film version. We worked closely together for about two years.

LG: He was advised by his friends and associates not to appear in *The Entertainer*. Do you know why he decided to do it?

TR: I think he felt instinctively that he had to change direction at that stage in his career. It was a time of release for him. He was breaking out of the world of Establishment theatre – and the world of Vivien Leigh. It was the first time in twelve or fifteen years that he wasn't playing with Vivien Leigh or directing her and himself. And it was the first time for ages that he had no other responsibilities than to be an actor. Of course the Establishment world that he had been involved with thought he was making a big mistake. They thought it was dangerous for him to associate himself with a group of people like myself and John Osborne and others at the Court, whom he didn't know much about and who were relatively inexperienced. I suppose from one narrow point of view it was dangerous and rash. But the instinct that told him he should change direction also took him in the right direction.

John Osborne once said that at the best moments in his career Larry has been able to an amazing extent to reflect the pulse and tempo – the quality and mood – of the nation. His performance in the film of *Henry* v caught that mood of patriotism and excitement – of hope for a brave new world – at the end of the last war.

Then before the war his performance in *Wuthering Heights* on the screen was completely in tune with that feeling at the end of the thirties that personal relationships were everything.

In *The Entertainer* his Archie Rice summed up the cynicism, the seediness, the moral compromises of the late fifties and the early sixties.

Of course he wasn't fully aware of what he was doing at the time. He was following his instinct as an artist – his intuition. And when he's done that in his career 'he's usually been right. But too often he has resisted it.

LG : You said that he was very helpful and generous to you when you were directing him in *The Entertainer* and that he was a joy to work with. But weren't there some difficulties and strain considering that he was being pulled in another direction by his friends and associates ?

TR : If his friends were telling him that he was jeopardizing his reputation by putting himself in the hands of a young untried director – and many of them were – he never gave the slightest indication that he thought so in his attitude to me. He was never the star actor guiding the tyro director. He was never patronizing or dictatorial. Our responsibility was to John Osborne and to doing the play as he had written it, and Larry accepted that. After the play opened at the Court he asked for certain changes. He wanted to cut a few things that he thought were politically unacceptable or in bad taste. He insisted that some of the cuts were made before we moved to the West End, but during rehearsals at the Court he was completely co-operative. However there was one difficult situation, which arose when it was suggested that Vivien Leigh should play the wife's part. We had to sit through a long discussion in the Connaught Hotel deciding whether or not she should wear a rubber mask because Larry thought she looked too beautiful for the part. Fortunately nothing came of that.

LG: Some of the critics at the time were surprised not only that he would accept the part of a third-rate, seedy, music-hall comic, but that he could play it so convincingly.

TR: They were underestimating his range, as they often have, and they were confining themselves to externals, as they often do. I think Larry understood Archie Rice from the very first moment. He could identify with the humour, the cynicism, the sentimentality of the man. Larry found it all within himself. He didn't start off with a very strong physical image of the part, as he often does. He is an exterior actor in the best sense of the word. He starts usually from some kind of outside observation, and he likes to build carefully so the performance becomes an artefact. And it's indestructible.

During rehearsals for *The Entertainer* there was one moment in the play that he was obviously afraid of. He was like a horse coming to a high fence and rearing away from it. It came at the end of the second act, and it was the moment when he heard of his son's death and he had to break down – collapse totally. When we were doing one of the last run-throughs he said: 'Tell me exactly what you think I should do – go through it step by step.' So I told him, but when we went into the run-through his genius took over and it was the most electrifying moment I've ever experienced in any rehearsal. It was extra-ordinary, unforgettable. George Relph, who was playing the Father, and who had played so much with Larry, said: 'I know these moments when his genius takes over. It happened when we were doing *Oedipus* and he discovered that shattering, tragic cry.'

Larry knew he'd done it again, but then we got to the dress rehearsal and Vivien Leigh came to see it. He became very nervous because of her; she seemed to have that effect on him at that time. And when we came to that big moment at the end of the second act he tried something similar but it wasn't so good, and she criticized it. The first time he'd allowed his feeling, his instinct, to guide him, but he couldn't do it again with the same power and intensity. So just before the first night we sent everyone away and we worked it all out technically – step by step. We repeated everything he'd done the first time, including all the gestures, movements, pauses. In other words we did a technical representation of the moment he'd discovered in emotion. We succeeded up to a point, but of course it was never quite so good as it had been in that electrifying rehearsal.

I remember he said to me towards the end of the run in New York that he thought he'd played the part full out – completely exposed – only three times in the whole run of about two years. That is part of his greatness – his absolute honesty about his own work. And it should be remembered that when he's not playing on true feeling and emotion, when he's not playing full out, he's such a superb craftsman and technician that he's always able to give a marvellous representation.

LG: Did you encounter any special difficulties when you were directing him in the film version of *The Entertainer*?

TR: None as far as he was concerned. He's a master of the technique of screen acting and he adjusted his performance perfectly from one medium to the other. But I don't think that anything written by John Osborne ever makes an ideal film because it's so essentially theatrical. Consequently filming *The Entertainer* had to be in some ways a compromise.

LG: The next time you worked with Olivier was in 1962, when you directed him in *Semi-Detached*. That wasn't one of his successes, was it?

TR: I'm afraid not. It was a complete contrast to *The Entertainer* and so was his mood and approach. He had been, as I said, marvellously co-operative and enthusiastic when we were doing *The Entertainer* but when we did *Semi-Detached* he seemed to be in a very depressed state of mind. It wasn't a great play to start with; it was a satire of sorts about the up-

As Malvolio in *Twelfth Night*, 1954.

As Titus Andronicus with Vivien Leigh as Lavinia, 1955.

As Archie Rice with Alan Bates as Frank in the film of *The Entertainer* (Osborne), 1960.

As Bassanes with Keith Michell as Ithocles in *The Broken Heart* (Ford), 1962.

As Astrov in *Uncle Vanya* (Chekov), 1963.

As Othello with Maggie Smith as Desdemona, 1964.

As Halvard Solness with Joan Plowright as Hilda Wangel in *The Master Builder* (Ibsen), 1964.

As Tattle in *Love for Love* (Congreve), 1965.

and-coming consumer man, the con man, the car salesman. The only point in Larry playing the part was that he should do it with tremendous relish and energy – with a certain kind of cockiness – which he can do very well. But he got the idea that the character was more restrained and Chekhovian. He had seen some man on the train to Brighton or somewhere whom he thought looked the part, and he wanted to play it in downbeat old clothes with a wig that made him look about twenty years older, whereas in everyone else's opinion he should have looked as young as he could.

But I'm afraid he'd got this conception of the part into his head and nobody could change it. I tried, but failed completely. So did his wife, Joan. So did everyone concerned with the production. We all knew it was a misconception but nothing could be done.

Then when the play opened it was clear that the audiences didn't like it. And he knew himself it wasn't working, but somehow he couldn't break out of the misconception. It was very odd and unusual for him. He seemed to be buried under a false image and he hadn't the energy, or the will, to free himself.

I think he had too much on his plate at that time. He was involved in intense preparations for the National Theatre: he was over-extended and fatigued.

LG: Why do you think he did *Semi-Detached* in the first place?

TR: It had been done originally at Nottingham, where it had been an enormous success with Leonard Rossiter playing the main part. It was one of those parts that are supposed to be Molièresque and the play was supposed to be Molièresque in construction. Anyway it had acquired a big reputation in Nottingham, but I suspect it was one of those productions that the critics love when they see it out of town, but they might have been less enthusiastic if it had been done initially in London. Unfortunately any energy Larry had to spare at the time went into getting the Nottingham accent right, and of course the accent didn't really matter a damn.

LG: I don't want to dwell on the subject of his failures – and there have been remarkably few in a long career, except in the early stages. But before we leave the subject, what do you think have been the others?

TR: There have been very few like *Semi-Detached*, which failed with the critics and the public, and it becomes very much a matter of personal taste and opinion. His Othello, for example, was hailed by some of the critics and it could be called one of his successes, but for me it was a flop. I didn't like it at all. He based his performance entirely on an external image – an image of a NEGRO in capital letters that became a degrading image. He concentrated too much on all the external details and not on the feelings of the man, and the result in my view was a bad Othello.

Another of his failures in Shakespeare was, I think, *Hamlet*. He's just not a Hamlet. He doesn't do introspection well and Hamlet without that is no good. I must say, too, that although he's tackled a wide range of parts and styles during his career he's not – surprisingly enough – capable of doing fast changes of mood in one performance. He can do them all but he cannot do the transitions from one to the other quickly. In other words he can play all the notes but he hasn't got the facility to run from one to the other rapidly in the way that Paul Scofield and Nicol Williamson can. The ability to do that is essential for an outstanding Hamlet.

LG: Apart from Archie Rice in *The Entertainer*, which of his performances has impressed you most?

TR: Without doubt Richard III. It was outstanding, a revelation to me of what a great actor can achieve. Next I'd place his Dr Astrov in *Uncle Vanya* and then his Captain in *The Dance of Death*. I think his Titus was memorable and so was his Macbeth. And I liked him very much in one of the classic comic parts in *The Way of The World*.

Undoubtedly he's a great comic actor but I don't want to get involved in making comparisons or drawing distinctions between his achievements in comedy and in tragedy. Certainly he's a very active man and comedy involves action, whereas tragedy needs passivity and he's not very good at that.

I think he can play deep disillusionment – a kind of black-
ness – as he did in *Titus* and to a certain extent in *Macbeth*.
Perhaps it's not deep tragic suffering but it's that moment after
suffering when there is a blank, hopeless despair. However the
trouble about comparing tragic and comic acting is that conceptions change with the times – particularly conceptions of
tragedy. Nowadays I'm not sure that tragedy has any meaning
for us in the sense it used to have. I mean life has gone beyond
tragedy.

People have seen so much that individual tragedy in the
Aristotelian sense – in the sense in which it was used over the
last three hundred years – is something that we do not understand any more, or even sympathize with. So I think the dis-
tinction between comedy and tragedy is rather a false one in
these times. Besides, in one part, like Archie Rice, for example,
Larry had to play comedy and what could be called tragedy,
and he did both superbly.

LG: Omitting *The Entertainer* again, which of his films do you
regard as the best?

TR: Unhesitatingly *Wuthering Heights*, in which he gave one
of the great romantic performances of the screen. The director,
Willie Wyler, directed him in another film, *Sister Carrie*, in
which he gave another marvellous performance that has always
for some reason been vastly underrated. You could see in it
the film blueprint for his later stage performance in *The Dance
of Death*.

LG: What do you think of his Shakespearean films?

TR: I wasn't impressed by his *Hamlet* for the reasons I've mentioned, and I think his *Richard* III wasn't nearly as successful
on the screen as it was on the stage. As I've said before, his
performance in *Henry* V was unforgettable, but I don't think
much of the film otherwise. Apart from his performance the
acting is abominable – atrocious in fact. The battle scene, which
was based on Eisenstein, is pathetic, especially if you compare
it with the original. Indeed the whole concept of the film,

starting with the Elizabethan theatre and all that, was in my view really awful – very bad as a piece of cinema. And he must take the blame as the director.

LG: What's your opinion of his work generally, as a director in films and in the theatre?

TR: I don't think he's a very good director in either medium. Of course he hasn't done very much in films except the Shakespearean ones and *The Prince and the Showgirl*, I think, but none of them has succeeded in terms of direction.

In the theatre I haven't really been impressed by anything he's done except *Uncle Vanya*, which was exceptionally fine. It may be prejudice on my part but I think there are very few actors who are good directors – although it's true that lots of good directors started their careers as actors.

However it's also true that great star actors like Olivier always get to a point when they long to direct themselves. They all want to be actor-managers at some period in their careers, and one of the difficulties is that they have other interests at heart in addition to the conception of the play.

However much they want to be fair to the other members of the cast they have a feeling deep down inside them that their performances will be enough. I think there's an element of this in varying degrees in all actor-managers. In Larry's case it may be a controllable, reasonable degree, but it's there nevertheless. For example, if as Olivier you play Othello and you have Frank Finlay as Iago, then you're revealing it. I don't mean that Finlay is a bad actor next to whom Olivier shines all the brighter. In fact Finlay is a very good actor, but he's on a completely different scale from Olivier. With Finlay playing Iago on his scale there has to be a different Othello from Olivier's.

In fairness to him, however, it should be said that more than most great star actors, he has tried to be part of an ensemble. But finally I'm afraid he finished up creating an actor-manager's company at the National.

LG: Does that mean that you disapprove of the policy he's followed during his reign at the National?

TR: Yes, I do disapprove. When he's had the Gielguds, the Scofields, the Finneys he's never played with them. It's never been on equal terms and they've never been built into an ensemble. I think it was criminal, for example, to let someone like Finney go from the National. Anyway it happened and with others, too, and Larry finished up with relatively minor actors merely surrounding him.

Still, it should be remembered that running a theatre is the most exhausting and taxing job in the world. I worked with George Devine at the Court for years, and I know it ultimately killed him. In a subtle way – certainly in a creative sense – it's been killing Larry. However much energy you have it's finally eaten up by coping with financial problems, management problems, quarrels with the press, quarrels with the board and so on. You have to waste time on trivial backstage rows, advising members of the cast about their personal problems, worrying about petty technical details. You can't keep it up for year after year and still produce your best creative work, and maintain the same degree of enthusiasm.

So I'm delighted that Larry finally decided to retire as artistic director and I hope from now on he'll concentrate entirely on acting.

LG: It's often been said that it's a mistake to have a national theatre at all. What are your views?

TR: I think there's something awful about the idea of a museum theatre which is what a national theatre tends to be – a theatre to present the great works of the past as though they're dead things. The real impulse of life in the theatre is aroused when a group of people get together to create something new. Still there may be a case for trying to build up a great repertory theatre, but usually the great repertory theatres have been founded on the work of one dramatist, like the Berliner Ensemble and Brecht.

One of the problems in this country is that there isn't a

sufficiently unified dramatic tradition to build on unless you confine yourself to Shakespeare. That's a perfectly reasonable basis for a theatre, but since it's entirely in the past it does limit you. You tend to become like the Comédie Française, however much you try to revitalize, and even allowing for the fact that Shakespeare is a universal dramatist who is capable of fresh interpretation in every age. So to sum up, I think the concept of a national theatre is wrong, and so far that's been proved.

What's so disappointing is that it hasn't at any time produced the electricity it could have produced if all the great stars we have – or some of them – had worked together, combining their talents.

LG: Didn't that happen up to a point at the Old Vic in the season at the end of the war?

TR: Yes it did when Larry, Ralph Richardson, Sybil Thorndike and others played so marvellously together. And it worked for a time at Stratford under Peter Hall. Perhaps it will happen again with him at the National. But whatever happens no one should allow Larry to do anything except act. Few, if any, can do that so well.

William Gaskill

LOGAN GOURLAY: Had you any contact with Olivier before you joined the National Theatre at its inception?

WILLIAM GASKILL: Only as a member of the audience. I wasn't working at the Royal Court when he appeared there in *The Entertainer*. When Larry knew he was going to run the National he asked George Devine to leave the Court and work with him. They were close personal friends and they had been during the period of Larry's divorce from Vivien Leigh and his marriage to Joan Plowright, who of course had been one of George's protégés at the Court. On the professional level Larry was very keen that some of the work George had done at the Court should be carried on at the National. They had many talks about it but George always said: 'Now wait a minute. I could never really be second in command.'

Larry tried to find some kind of compromise, but by that time George was a sick man and not long after he died. At that stage Larry quite simply thought the next best thing would be to have two directors whom George had trained – John Dexter and myself.

I believe Joan Plowright and Ken Tynan thought so too. Joan felt that Larry shouldn't have too many people of his own generation around him, but should have some younger people who would bring a new stimulus to the founding of the National. A very sensible idea.

It took him a long time, however, to persuade me to join him. He used to talk jokingly about 'the wooing of Billy Gaskill'. He used to say: 'I've spent more money wooing you than I've ever spent wooing a woman. I'm always taking you out to expensive lunches and you still haven't said yes.'

LG: Why were you reluctant to say yes?

WG: I'm not exactly sure. But I think that having been largely reared at the Court with George Devine I wanted to be sure that the National, as the Court had done, would put an emphasis on modern work.

Unfortunately it hasn't, of course, and perhaps a national theatre never can. But that was what preoccupied me at the 'wooing' period. Anyway it was a strange and flattering experience.

LG: Did the wooing include promises that the National *would* put on new work and not be just a theatrical museum?

WG: Yes. The intention – the plans – were there, though it hasn't quite worked out that way. I think Larry has a strong chameleon quality. I'm sure most people who know him would agree. He has the ability to change and to adapt himself very quickly to the people he's with – even to people of a new generation. He found it much easier for example to be assimilated into a production at the Royal Court than John Gielgud did. In fact it took Gielgud about ten years longer than Larry even to get around to doing a production at the Court.

Larry's awareness of the movement of the times has always been very acute, but sometimes, I'm afraid, not always very sincere – not always for the right reasons.

LG: John Osborne says that Olivier tries too hard to keep up with the times and that his anxiety not to be thought old-hat is sometimes too desperate.

WG: I think that's true.

LG: Do you think the artistic climate in this country makes it difficult to have a national theatre that isn't just a museum?

WG: I don't think the climate is any worse for it here than anywhere else. But it's no better either and I'm afraid our National has only too readily become very much like a continental state theatre. It's difficult to know how you can have the right vision for a national theatre. You can have a vision for a new theatre. Or you can have a writer like Brecht, for instance, who wants to make his own company and do his own plays, and at a certain time the opportunity occurs for him to create an ensemble.

If you asked Larry what he tried to create an ensemble for he would probably repeat the phrase that Ken Tynan hands out about 'showing a spectrum of the world drama'. It sounds fine, but every other theatre shows a spectrum of world drama. There isn't actually a very specific impulse in that aim – an impulse that would create something that would be endlessly interesting. Not that any company can be endlessly interesting, I'm afraid. Any ensemble has a limit of life; and the impulse of any individuals working in it has a limit of life. The energy with which you create a new theatre has a short life span. Even George Devine at the Court didn't have a long span. And I'm afraid he stayed in the theatre beyond the time when his enthusiasm was real and fresh.

However I must admit that it was all very exciting at the National at the beginning. There was the excitement of creating a new company – choosing actors and bringing them together, doing one or two plays that were different from the usual choice for national theatres – and of course being in a working relationship with an actor whom I respected greatly, and who was the greatest living English actor.

But when I finally realized that the end product wasn't going to be largely different from the continental state theatres I lost my interest and enthusiasm. I was there for only two years and at first the work was stimulating and rewarding, but I realized that it wasn't going to develop into something more rewarding.

However, like any theatre of its kind the National will from time to time renew itself. And given new blood it will revitalize itself. New blood is essential. I don't think anyone – even someone as gifted as Larry Olivier – should go on running the same theatre for more than five years. I myself was at the Court for seven years and I suspect that was two years too long. And as

I said a moment ago, I think George Devine stayed on too long.

The essential thing – the pouring-in of new ideas – can be done by one person only for a limited period of time. Then you have to get away to renew yourself. There comes a point inevitably when it becomes a kind of treadmill, and if you stay on it's for the wrong reasons. You say to yourself, for example: ' It's my theatre, after all – I helped to create it – and I should stay with it.' That's when you should get out fast.

However Larry at the National was a special case. He may have felt like getting out sooner, but at the same time he had a very strong desire to stay on for the opening of the new theatre on the South Bank. A very understandable desire.

LG: You say that no one should run a theatre for more than five years, but doesn't it have to be the right five years in terms of it being a period when the artistic climate is right, when the acting and writing talents are available? Diaghilev, for example, couldn't have created his ballet theatre if the right artists and composers hadn't been available at that time.

WG: I do think Diaghilev is a false model for anyone in the theatre. No one has ever pulled it off like Diaghilev, but he did operate in a peculiar kind of hot-house climate and he was constantly seeking the new and the experimental. He was always getting bored with, say, Picasso and moving on to Miró, or Max Ernst, or whoever.

It's true you can sometimes sense a certain climate and take advantage of the talents that are flourishing in that climate. Larry, I think, sensed that when he was starting his new National company the strong creative theatrical elements in the climate of that time were at the Royal Court, and so he invited us to join him. Unfortunately things didn't work out as we'd hoped. I think finally that, if Larry and I were being quite truthful, we'd agree that his vision and mine didn't fully come together, though there were lots of points of contact.

LG: When you were working there as a director with Olivier as the supreme director, as it were, did you get on well together?

WG: Yes, we did generally. However the only time I ever directed him in a production – *The Recruiting Officer* – I don't think he enjoyed himself at all. In fact I think he hated it.

LG: Why particularly?

WG: To begin with I was doing a lot of improvisation and he went along with it because he's very game about that sort of thing, but he clearly didn't like it. Indeed I suspect he thought it was a load of rubbish. I'm afraid we never quite hit a good working relationship as director and actor.

LG: Is he a difficult actor to work with from a director's point of view because, for example, his vast experience gives him strong preconceptions about the play and his part?

WG: He didn't have any preconceptions in this case. The truth is that he didn't know how to play the part. He didn't arrive saying: 'This is how I'm going to play it.' On the contrary he was very much at sea, and would have admitted so at the time. In other productions, of course, he does arrive fully prepared, knowing exactly what he intends to do.

The *Othello*, for instance, was fascinating. He knew all the lines in advance and at the very first reading he actually played the part with all the stops out. It was an extraordinary occasion. All the other actors were standing about with their scripts and there was the star playing the part as though it were the first night.

Sometimes when I'm asked what makes a great actor I'm tempted to say simply knowing all his lines at the beginning of rehearsals. The important point is that if you want to produce the kind of force and energy an Olivier can produce in the finished performance, the preparation is everything. All the great actors and actresses I've worked with have always done a great deal of homework. Edith Evans and Maggie Smith, for example, arrive at the first rehearsal with a lot of work already done on their parts. I think it's essential to do this, particularly if you're tackling a big classical role. You can't hope just to muddle through in rehearsals.

LG: Were you involved in any way in the *Othello* production?

WG: No, not directly. But everyone in the company was interested and I used to watch the rehearsals whenever I had the chance. When you work alongside someone like Olivier you feel: 'Ah, here is someone who is really practising his craft.' I'm afraid there are very few actors nowadays who really practise their craft. It's remarkable to watch someone like Olivier, who actually prepares step by step how he will walk on to the stage – how he will handle each prop. I was seduced by the dedication and conscientiousness he brought to his work.

I'm very sorry that we didn't hit it off when we were doing *The Recruiting Officer*. Perhaps I was to blame. Perhaps I should have approached him quite differently – in a straightforward technical way. But because among other things he was playing a supporting part, I had an idea that he should feel the sense of the ensemble – the way we were working and improvising. I think he understood what I was after, though he never quite caught it.

LG: You said you were improvising a great deal. Did that mean he didn't have a basis on which to exercise his craft?

WG: That's right. I took away the usual things that he would have to work on. He's very concerned with bits of business and props and he likes to work out every movement and gesture. He even gets his wigs ready well in advance. He transforms himself by the make-up and the physical mannerisms he adopts.

I remember seeing him early on in rehearsals having his wig fitted. His make-up was marvellous, as always, but I'm afraid in this case he never quite felt how the part ought to be played. And I never succeeded in conveying it to him. However, people liked his performance very much. It was highly praised. But I thought it was one of his less successful performances.

LG: During your two years at the National how much professional contact did you have with him apart from the production of *The Recruiting Officer*?

WG: We were very close in a way. We used to meet all the time to discuss the choice of plays, the casting and so on. He was very receptive to ideas in those days and he wasn't particularly autocratic. Sometimes he'd stand firm on relatively small things, but in general he didn't try to impose his will on everything.

LG: Could you sum up in a few words what you think are his outstanding qualities as an actor?

WG: There's his craftsmanship of course – his attention to detail – but I suppose the outstanding impression I'm left with is his energy.

My memories are of those moments when he projects his energy outwards – in speaking, for example, when he hurls a line as if it were a javelin. He has the ability to take his voice and actually throw it, knowing exactly where it will go, which is something that Gielgud, for instance, has never been able to do. One example was when he took that line 'Farewell the tranquil mind . . .' [Othello] and delivered it in a totally original way. It may have been the wrong interpretation but it was very effective. As you know, it's usually done as a sad, reflective, contemplative speech, but he did it on a note of attacking frenzy, which was bold and arresting.

I think, however, that all his qualities as an actor were seen at their best, not in a classical play, but in *The Entertainer*. There was a lot of talk at the time to the effect that a more emotional actor would have been better in the part. Rubbish, I think.

There is a certain kind of actor, like the late Wilfrid Lawson and some continental actors, who have tremendous inner warmth. I've seen Archie Rice played more emotionally by one of those actors and it just didn't come off. There's something about the man having to entertain regardless of what he's feeling that Larry captured, and which is essentially what the play is about.

Larry had a complete understanding of the role. In an odd way he knew it was about him. I remember we had an evening at the Old Vic for the George Devine award when various actors came along to do their pieces. Naturally enough, Larry's was from *The Entertainer*. People were sitting around in their costumes as they do on those occasions and suddenly right behind us in the stalls there was the face of Archie Rice – that peculiar mask – and Larry was leaning forward saying : 'This is really me, isn't it?' And it was him absolutely. That kind of heartless clown's mask is very much part of Larry Olivier.

I don't mean that he's cold and unemotional, but at the same time I think it's sentimental to expect him, because he is an outstanding actor, to be a man of great feeling and emotional depth. Not many actors are.

Actresses are sometimes different. Someone like Sybil Thorndike, for instance, has deep feeling and understanding that come from the heart and convey themselves to an audience. Generally actors aren't like that. They are more hollow. I don't think anyone should be surprised or shocked by this. It's very much part of what makes an actor. He's a man who puts on masks. The characters he plays sometimes have more solidity and reality than he has himself : they are the substance and he is the shadow.

LG : You have compared Olivier once or twice with Gielgud. Do you think, as some people have said, that Gielgud can be more moving and convincing in the great tragic parts like Lear and Hamlet?

WG : I shall probably never see a better Hamlet than Gielgud's, but that was because of those quick-thinking, brilliantly flexible qualities of his, not because he was intensely moving. I can't say that I've ever been particularly moved by John on the stage any more than I've been moved by Larry. Neither of them has made me shed a tear. John sheds a lot of tears himself and Larry sheds none, but I don't think either of them move the audience profoundly.

I think Larry is a great heroic actor 'rather than a tragic actor. I thought his Coriolanus was heroically splendid. When he did that speech beginning, 'There is a world elsewhere . . .', I was amazed the audience didn't stand up and cheer. It was done so brilliantly – with such authority and panache.

He's always been very good playing men of action like

Coriolanus and Henry v. But he's never been quite so good playing the contemplative, reflective, introspective characters like Hamlet.

I regret very much not having seen his Hotspur, another of the heroic parts. He introduced that business of Hotspur having trouble with his 'Ws' and stuttering over them. The next person to play it was Michael Redgrave and he did it with a Northumberland accent that was largely incomprehensible. Then when Roy Dotrice got round to doing it he used a Scots accent with a kilt and tam-o'-shanter. By that time I thought the whole point of the character had disappeared and I longed to see a heroic Hotspur again like Larry's.

LG: Do you think he will go down to posterity as one of the giants of the English theatre like Kean and Irving?

WG: Yes, I'm sure he will. Until Olivier came along there hadn't been an actor of tremendous stature on the English stage since Irving's time. Olivier was the first to seize the imagination of the public as the leading actor of his generation.

I have a dream that the actors like Irving and Kean were more powerful and compelling than anyone today, including Olivier, but it's an idle dream. There's no way of knowing. At least future generations will get some indication of Olivier's acting from what's preserved on film.

LG: What do you think of his film work?

WG: I loved *Henry v*. I saw it first when I was at school and I went to see it again and again. Incidentally, I've found it very strange at times to be working with people like Olivier who were mythical figures in my childhood. I suppose in a way I've never quite got over that kind of fan attitude, however critical I might have become on occasions when I came to work with him.

Of the other two Shakespearean films I did not like his *Hamlet* very much and I disliked his *Richard III*, in which I think he was trying to repeat the success of *Henry v*, and failing totally.

Among the non-Shakespearean films *The Entertainer* was

much less successful than the play, mainly because it was so difficult to transfer from the stage to the new medium.

One of the most successful of all his film performances was in *Wuthering Heights*. I'll never forget one particular scene – the one in which he tells Isabella, played by Geraldine Fitzgerald, that he doesn't love her. He was cold-eyed and ruthless – completely compelling. He excels in moments like that.

LG: Of all the parts he's played in Shakespearean and modern drama is there one you would select as the most outstanding and impressive?

WG: Without hesitation Archie Rice in *The Entertainer*. Of course he's given many memorable performances over the years, but nothing he's done, including some of his highly praised performances at the National, has impressed me quite so much as his Archie Rice.

LG: You said earlier that you lost your interest and enthusiasm for the National when you saw that it was developing along the lines of the continental state theatres. Was there any specific reason that made you finally break away from Olivier and the National?

WG: One of the main reasons was that I thought Ken Tynan's influence on Larry and the theatre had become professionally bad. Ken has very strong commercial instincts – and so has Larry of course – but at least Larry doesn't try to behave like a Broadway producer. I found that very tiresome and misguided. I felt finally that I might as well be working on Broadway with a producer saying: 'Aw, Jesus, baby, that's not right. You gotta cut a bit here, baby.'

The final showdown came at a meeting in Larry's house when we were discussing the plans for the next season. Ken suddenly started to talk about the need for more stars. I objected and said to Larry: 'I can understand that you have to rely on Ken's advice about the choice of plays. But I don't think in any circumstances he should be allowed to dictate the choice of actors. That's not his business as literary manager.'

As Edgar with Geraldine McEwan as Alice in the film of *The Dance of Death* (Strindberg), 1968. This wedding photograph was constructed from pictures taken when he was 25 and she was 22.

Rehearsing as Field-Marshal Sir John French for the film *Oh What A Lovely War*, 1969.

As Plucheux in *A Flea in Her Ear* (Feydeau), 1967 (previous page).

As Mr Creakle in the film *David Copperfield* (Dickens), 1969.

As Shylock in *The Merchant of Venice*, 1970.

As James Tyrone
in *Long Day's
Journey into
Night* (O'Neill),
1971.

As Andrew
Wyke with
Michael Caine
as Milo Tindle
in the film of
Sleuth (Anthony
Shaffer), 1972.

With Kenneth
Tynan from a
model by Roger
Law.

It developed into a big row and I'm afraid I got very angry. Larry left the room and went upstairs. He reappeared about half an hour later and said: 'I have to tell you that I must have Ken involved in *all* these discussions.'

It was at that point that I knew it was no good going on. I couldn't work in that kind of set-up.

LG: Did Olivier have any particular reasons for involving Tynan in all his decisions at the National?

WG: I've no idea why he became so dependent professionally on Tynan. Fortunately, however, it stopped short of total dependence because, for example, Ken suggested that Larry should resign over a minor issue like whether or not *The Soldiers*, that play involving Churchill's reputation, should be put on at the National.

Apart from any other aspect of the issue it was a dreadful play that didn't deserve to be put on at the National or anywhere else.

The significant thing is that Ken, who started all the fuss about putting the play on, didn't resign himself. I'm afraid that all the decisions he has taken or caused to be taken, particularly about the choice of plays, have been decisions that have led the theatre to be just another national theatre – another Comédie Française.

One of these decisions was to bring over Charon to do the Feydeau farce *A Flea in Her Ear*. Now there's nothing intrinsically wrong with inviting Charon to do Feydeau, but you're not creating an individual national theatre in this way. All you're doing is importing a ready-made property from elsewhere. You're not developing a native style in a native theatre of your own – which is what a national theatre should be doing. And, remember, if you have a British National Theatre you're in the peculiarly advantageous situation of having almost more plays than you need. No other country in the world has as large a national repertoire of plays as Britain. Apart from Shakespeare there is an enormous wealth of material to draw on.

But I'm afraid to me Ken Tynan has always been one for

the quick trendy ideas like importing *A Flea in Her Ear* or *Front Page*, which, funnily enough, often turn out to be rather old-fashioned and reactionary ideas.

LG: What kind of working relationship did Tynan have with Olivier?

WG: It's difficult to say exactly. Whatever it was I don't think it had anything to do with affection or real fellow-feeling. But I may be wrong. Perhaps in a sense Larry did have a fellow-feeling for Ken. Perhaps there is something similar between them. Ken, for example, can kick you in the teeth one day and ring you up the next as though nothing had happened to ask you to do something for him. You're so staggered by his doing it that you forget to remind him of what he did the day before: you're overcome by the outrageous cheek. Now I think Larry has a bit of that too, so they do have something in common.

LG: It has been said that their professional relationship had certain Shakespearean parallels, and that it could be called an Othello–Iago relationship with Olivier as Othello.

WG: No, I don't agree. They're both Iago. Neither is a natural Othello, I can tell you that. They used to say wounding Iago-like things about each other behind each other's back. Yet Larry would rush to Ken's support, as he did when I had that showdown with them about Ken's influence on casting.

Obviously the relationship was a very complex one and I wouldn't attempt to analyse it. In fairness it did produce momentary things of some value, but it didn't produce first-class sustained work in a first-class national theatre. And I do think Ken's influence is a great deal to blame. Someone else could perhaps have helped Larry to create a set-up in which, for one thing, he could have acted more – as he should have done.

I think it's terribly sad that Larry didn't appear with John Gielgud when John was there. It's tragic really that the opportunity was missed. On the most traditional level one of the excitements that a national theatre should provide is the opportunity to see great star performers playing together – doing their stuff together. That's the kind of electricity a national theatre can, and should, generate.

Again they had Paul Scofield there, but Larry didn't do anything with him. That was stupid too. If nothing else the public has a right to expect star ensemble playing from the National. If you're not going to have a true ensemble, then for God's sake, let's at least have some fireworks.

Under Larry – influenced by Ken – it's been an actor-manager's theatre tempered by some acknowledgements to the Charons, the Zeffirellis and the Bergmans.

I'm not objecting to Larry doing his stuff in a few big parts – no one would object to that – but I do object to the pretence that it was an ensemble company. It wasn't. It was a spurious kind of ensemble, and it didn't have the glamour of old-fashioned actor-manager's theatre about it. It fell between the two stools.

Apart from Larry the company just wasn't strong enough. At the opening it was stronger, but it dwindled in strength over the years and on all levels. Looking back I think the National might have been better if someone like George Devine or Peter Hall had been involved from the beginning. But that's idle speculation. Larry thought he was the man for the job and in a sense he was the right kind of figurehead. But what he didn't have was the right kind of vision to maintain a long-term concept of what a national theatre should be.

He saw himself as the heir to Irving, Garrick and Kean. He's always thought of himself as that, and he consciously picked up the threads – almost self-consciously. For example, he has a little private museum with Kean's sword and other pieces. That's typical Larry.

But today's National Theatre must avoid museum associations and it should not be run by Irving's or Kean's successor. Of course Larry has never been quite an actor-manager in the way that these historic figures were. The age of that kind of dominant actor-manager is over. It died about fifty years ago. But the memory lingers on, particularly in Larry's imagination.

He has a great nostalgia for it. You get the impression at times that he feels he is the actor-manager in the old, all-powerful style.

I remember on one occasion after a performance of *Othello* John Dexter gave the cast a lecture because he thought it had been a bad performance. He told them all off, including Larry, who was furious. He thought it was intolerable that he should have been criticized in front of his own company. Very much the attitude of the old actor-managers – and the wrong attitude if you claim to be building an ensemble company.

LG: How would he have taken the criticism from his director if it had been done privately?

WG: Very well. I know from personal experience that he will accept and listen to criticism. Great as he is – and aware as he is of his own greatness – he knows he is not beyond criticism.

Lady Lee

'Now is the winter of our discontent.' Always when I hear these opening lines from *Richard III* I see a sinister hunch-backed figure moving from the wings on to the stage. This for me was one of Laurence Olivier's greatest performances.

From my earliest theatre-going days I have been his fan, but there he was behind the footlights, and there I was an entranced member of the audience. It was much more recently, that is in the years between 1964 and 1970, when I was Minister for the Arts, that I saw another side of Olivier. I was concerned to see the National Theatre established. There had been so many delays; so many disappointments.

Laurence Olivier, a perfectionist, wanted a small national theatre so that everyone in the audience could have a perfect occasion. I was not convinced. We were discussing this together at an Arts Council reception when Henry Moore joined us. 'Larry,' he said, 'have you never been young?' This comment crystallized what I had been trying to say. It brought to my mind the most wonderful theatre-going occasion I had in my student days at Edinburgh University. There we were as young students, queueing up for the cheapest seats, and delighted beyond measure when we found ourselves climbing the long stairs to the gods. We were clinging like flies to the ceiling, but this was one of the last occasions on which Pavlova had performed.

So there it was. The actor, so outstandingly distinguished in his own job, wanted everyone in the audience to have a perfect occasion. The other argument for a larger hall was, of course, to enable more of the younger and poorer people to share in its delights.

I am not competent to pass judgement on Laurence Olivier as a theatre director and manager, but I do know that on the most important aspect of all he deeply impressed the Arts Council, the representatives from government departments and myself. Once plans for a National Theatre were at last going ahead, he came to see us to plead for a junior Vic. At that time he had recently recovered from a very serious illness, and we were all still apprehensive about his health. Whether this influenced Treasury representatives or not I cannot say, but what I do know is that when he had pleaded with us for a junior Vic, explaining that you cannot have a great national theatre on a star system alone, and that stars come and go, so that there must be a company, an ensemble, we were convinced. I was also conscious that great actors can be selfish, concerned only for themselves, but here was Laurence Olivier pleading for the talented young to be able to perform without straight away being exposed to the full glare of a national theatre and professional critics. At the end of the meeting I said to him: 'Please send me a letter setting down what you have just said.' This he did, and I promptly sent a copy to our prime minister, Mr Harold Wilson, and to my Treasury colleagues. I had been fighting so many battles with the Treasury that I had felt I could not press as hard as usual for this particular scheme, but I was willing enough to have a go. To my delight, almost by return of post, I received financial consent. This was entirely due to Laurence Olivier.

There is a very considerable difference between the skills needed on the stage and on the public platform. This was impressed upon me when our mutual friends, Constance Cummings and Ben Levy, said that Joan and Larry would like to come to the House of Lords when I was being introduced. The last thing I wanted to do was to collect an audience for this complex, medieval ceremony. But of course I said I would be delighted if they would be present as my guests. What I did not know until later was that Larry was treating this as a kind of dress rehearsal, and that he was more nervous about his introduction to the Lords than anyone I had ever known. At the time he wrote to me: 'Joanie and I were much troubled by the idea of my accepting a peerage for quite a time, but now I think we can probably face up to it, and only hope to God we can do something of good by it.'

Lord Olivier's Maiden Speech in the House of Lords*

Lord Olivier: My Lords, I have the honour to crave the indulgence of your Lordships' House. During the maiden speech which follows I fear your Lordships may find grim cause to reflect upon the prescient genius of the introducer of this tenderest of courtesies, and if I fail to achieve it then I must beg to suggest to your Lordships that it would be most contrary to the chivalry for which your Lordships' House is so famous to withhold your gallantry and refuse to indulge a maiden of 64.

I stand before your Lordships the second Baron of my name. The first, incomparably much more deserving, virtuous, illustrious, and in service to his country richer than I can ever hope to be, was my uncle, twice Governor of Jamaica, K.C.M.G., friend to Bernard Shaw, the Webbs, and all the eminent Socialists of the day with whom he created the Fabian Society. He entered your Lordships' House the first Labour Peer – he seems to have started quite a thing. He served the Government in 1925 as Secretary for India, a title once representing one of the richest jewels in the Imperial Crown and which now sounds perhaps almost quaint to the retrenched ears whose lobes can only boast the holes to show where once such lush gems hung.

But it is not on account of being my uncle's nephew that I am here, no matter what storybook feudal nostalgia might tempt me to allow you to think so. The fact of my presence can only find reason in what his enemies would describe as his

* Extracted from *Hansard* for 20 July 1971.

greatest eccentricity, his friends as the only eccentricity of which our recent Prime Minister was ever culpable. For a time I resisted this honour, as I thought was proper and to be expected, I think, in a person of my calling; the breaking of ice in any sense being apt to cause hesitation in most of us. But it does not take all that multi-repeated persuasion, that seethingly passionate ardour to make even the coyest maiden of 64 to wonder what on earth she thinks it is she has got to lose. He, Mr Wilson, said he wanted people like me to have a forum. . . .

My Lords, I believe in Great Britain and in keeping her great under the Sovereign. My 'great' is not rhetorical: it refers directly to the continuance of the family of England and Scotland, Wales and Northern Ireland, together with what relationships we can still muster among those peoples with whom, if we lose a relation, we gain a friend. I am proud to belong to this family. The trend of nationalistic feelings has now spread, we are given to understand, to Cornwall. Sometimes it seems to me that we shall be lucky if, when that superb building at present half erected at the foot of Waterloo Bridge on the South Bank finally achieves its sky-line, we shall dare to inscribe a legend more boastful than 'The National Theatre of Surrey'. Here my profession must own a debt of incalculable magnitude to the noble and chivalrous Viscount, Lord Chandos, and the noble Lord, Lord Cottesloe, together with most grateful acknowledgements to the G.L.C. for their tireless efforts in creating this new 'London Pride'.

I believe in the theatre; I believe in it as the first glamourizer of thought. It restores dramatic dynamics and their relationships to life size. I believe that in a great city, or even in a small city or a village, a great theatre is the outward and visible sign of an inward and probable culture. I believe in the Common Market, in the Concorde, in Foulness and the Brighton Belle. I believe in any thing that will keep our domains, not wider still and wider, but higher still and higher in the expectancy and hope of quality and probity.

I humbly thank your Lordships for your kind attention.

Some Reviews

THE TAMING OF THE SHREW: The Shrew was boldly and vigorously played, with dark flashing eyes and a spiteful voice.
Birmingham Post, 2 April 1922

MARY QUEEN OF SCOTS: Mr Laurence Olivier's Bothwell is an excellently conceived and executed portrait except that I think he is a little too light, especially in the voice which has the tennis-club, will-you-serve-first-partner-or-shall-I ring about it.
Sunday Times, 8 January 1934

BIOGRAPHY: Mr Olivier is 'werry fierce' throughout, and I foresee that his continuous ill-temper will make him a matinee-idol for masochists. *Sunday Times, 29 April 1934*

ROMEO AND JULIET: Mr Laurence Olivier can play many parts. Romeo is not one of them. His voice has neither the tone nor the compass and his blank verse is the blankest I ever heard.
When Miss Ashcroft asked him 'Wherefore art thou Romeo?' I was inclined to echo her question.
Mr Gielgud was the Mercutio of tradition. He lived like a rake and died like a gentleman – all too soon for my liking.
Evening Standard, 18 October 1935

Mr Olivier's Romeo suffered enormously from the fact that the spoken poetry of the part eluded him. In his delivery he brought off a twofold inexpertness which approached virtuosity – that of gabbling all the words in a line and uttering each line as a staccato whole cut off from its fellows. *Sunday Times, 20 October 1935*

I have seen few sights so moving as the spectacle of Mr Olivier's Romeo, stunned with Juliet's beauty, fumbling for words with which to say his love. This impetuous boy, struggling to be articulate, is the expression at once of his own mumness and of the mumness that still clogged his creator's pen. I am not bold enough to say what Shakespeare would or would not have liked, but I think his eyes would have shone had he seen this Romeo: young and ardent and full of clumsy grace. *Observer, 3 November 1935*

ROMEO AND JULIET: Mr Gielgud when he played this part gave us the cascade, but failed at the bluff; there is plenty of honest rock about Mr Olivier's Mercutio, though he turns on the poetry in the way that athletic young fellows turn on the morning bath. *The Times, 29 November 1935*

Now that John Gielgud and Laurence Olivier have changed parts, the production, which could hardly gain much in emotional effect, gains greatly in artistic balance. Mr Gielgud's Romeo is more romantic than was Mr Olivier's, has a much greater sense of the beauty of language, and substitutes a thoughtfulness that suits the part for an impetuosity that did not.

And if there were doubts whether Mr Olivier was well cast as Romeo, there can be none about his Mercutio. This is a brilliant piece of work – full of zest, humour and virility. The 'Queen Mab' speech – that most famous of purple patches – went for rather less than usual; but it could be counted well lost, seeing that it gave us a perfect interpretation of one of the most effective small parts in all drama. *Daily Telegraph, 29 November 1935*

BEES ON THE BOATDECK: Messrs Richardson and Olivier, who have jointly produced the piece, have given us a grand partnership in its performance. . . . I have not see Mr Olivier better than in the raillery and the comic invention of the second officer. Continually these two by delicacy of inflection or business, win their author an unconvenanted benefit of laughter. *Ivor Brown, Observer, 1936*

Mr Ralph Richardson and Mr Laurence Olivier having nothing to act, can only cover up poverty with fuss. And how poorly they do it! . . . Mr Olivier is even less happy, for his second officer is no second officer at all, but a young gentleman from behind the counter of a bank or stores. That his Bob should know enough about an anchor to outline it correctly on his forearm in semblance of a tattoo amazes me exceedingly. *James Agate, Sunday Times, 10 May 1936*

HENRY V: Laurence Olivier's Henry is not the hearty young Rugby forward with a leaning for poetry that we usually get. He is a man conscious of destiny, sober under the weight of responsibility. Mr Olivier has an extraordinary power these days of arriving at his top note early in a big speech, and maintaining it without effort to the end. It is a power that should be sparingly used, for if it develops into a mannerism it will be fatal. But it is most effective.

Daily Telegraph, 7 April 1937

OEDIPUS : I am to say here that first the producer's speech and then the Sheridan romp successfully dowsed whatever light I had seen the tragedy in. In the world of opera, where the sublime and the ridiculous are one, these grotesqueries of juxtaposition are not tolerated. At the end of *Tristan* no producer comes forward to thank Messrs Squills for the love-philtre, or Messrs Cordage and Wain for the new rigging. Nor, in that world, do they follow *Electra* with *The Pirates of Penzance*. I confess to finding Mr Olivier's Puff unhearable and unseeable in this contiguity. Would Irving have followed Hamlet with Jingle? No. And I departed, declining to entertain an Oedipus complex. Instead I found myself thinking about the Greek Chorus in a most un-Greek way. Had it been, I reflected with Groucho Marx, a case of one man with fifteen beards, or fifteen men wearing the same beard.

Sunday Times, 21 October 1945

RICHARD III: I remember being immensely impressed by this performance some four years ago; and I wondered, as I watched it the other night, whether the brilliance of much of it hadn't blinded me to its faults. For it no longer seems quite as good as it did; and since the brilliance has been so widely praised, perhaps it will not seem grudging to try now to trace the weakness. The marvellous opening speech of self-revelation is delivered by Olivier as perfectly as I remember it before. The edge on his voice is ice, and what has been frozen in Richard of Gloucester is that pity which enables the normal man to come to terms with the worst of his own defects. But this man cannot forgive himself his; sprouting into deformity as they are, he must flaunt them against the world. Having no mercy for himself, he has none for others; and his bitterness is displayed at its bleakest in a wintry sort of humour so sardonic, so pitiless, that it curdles our response.

But then, as the story moves, we bump up against what must be, given a great actor, the real difficulty in playing it. Exactly what kind of laughter is he to evoke in us? Very early on Sir Laurence seemed to me to be getting the wrong kind. The first time it happened I felt a pang of sympathy for him as an actor – he was being misunderstood by the more obvious-minded of his audience, who seemed to think Richard Crookback 'funny'. Not, that is to say, funny in some mordant, macabre way, but just ordinarily funny. I expected to hear him being careful next time to point the edge more sharply. But no, it comes again, and again, until one realizes that he is deliberately playing for that kind of ordinary laugh.

New Statesman & Nation, 16 February 1949

TITUS ANDRONICUS: As Lavinia, Miss Vivien Leigh receives the news that she is about to be ravished on her husband's corpse with little more than the mild annoyance of one who would have preferred foam rubber: otherwise the minor parts are played up to the hilt.

Sir Laurence Olivier's Titus, even with one hand gone, is a five-finger exercise transformed into an unforgettable concerto of grief. This is a performance which ushers us into the presence of one who is, pound for pound, the greatest actor alive. As usual he raises one's hair with the risks he takes: Titus enters not as a beaming hero but as a battered veteran, stubborn and shambling, long past caring about the people's cheers. A hundred campaigns have tanned his heart to leather, and from the cracking of that heart there issues a terrible music, not untinged by madness. One hears great cries, which, like all of this actor's best effects, seem to have been dredged up from an ocean-bed of fatigue. One recognized, though one had never heard it before, the noise made in its last extremity by the cornered human soul. We knew from his Hotspur and his Richard III that Sir Laurence could explode: now we know that he can suffer as well. All the grand unplayable parts, after this, are open to him – Skelton's *Magnificence*, Ibsen's *Brand*, Goethe's *Faust* – anything, so long as we can see those lion eyes search for solace, that great jaw sag. *Observer, 21 August 1955*

TWELFTH NIGHT: Remains Sir Laurence Olivier, whose sun peeped through the chintz curtains of the production and might, with any help, have blazed. Hints abounded of a wholly original Malvolio; a self-made snob, aspiring to consonance with the quality but ever betrayed by vowels from Golders Green; Malvolio was seen from his own point of view instead of (as usually) Sir Toby's. Yet the sketch remained as outline, a diverting exercise but hardly the substance of Sir L's vocation. *Observer, 24 April 1955*

MACBETH (Stratford-on-Avon): Sir Laurence Olivier's is the best Macbeth since – Macbeth's. His performance reminds one of the insolent magnificence of that Sunderland football 'team of all the talents' which, in a season just before the First World War, stayed at the bottom of the League all through September, and the following April finished at the top with a record number of points. For, it must be admitted, the opening scenes of Sir Laurence's Macbeth are bad; bad with the confident badness of a master who knows that he has miracles to come. ·

Harold Hobson, Sunday Times, 12 June 1955

CAESAR AND CLEOPATRA / ANTONY AND CLEOPATRA: In *Caesar and Cleopatra* she (Vivien Leigh) keeps a firm grip on the narrow ledge which is indisputably hers; the level on which she can be pert, sly and spankable and fill out a small personality. She does to the letter what Shaw asks of his Queen and not a semi-colon more. And how obsequiously Sir Laurence seems to play along with her, never once bowing to the command which most great actors hear, the command to enlarge on the flat symbols of the text.

Antony and Cleopatra is another world. This is a leaping giant of a play which assumes 'greatness' of its performers and sleeps under anything else.

'You were a boggler ever' says Antony at one point to his idle doxy, and one can feel Miss Leigh's imagination boggling at the thought of playing Cleopatra. Taking a deep breath and resolutely focusing her pert winkle charm, she launches another of her careful readings: ably and passionlessly she picks her way among its great challenges presenting a glibly mown lawn where her author had imagined a jungle.

Her confidence amazingly never flags. Once or twice in the evening the lines call for a sort of palatial sweetness; and she scents these moments and excels in them.

Yet one feeling rode over these in my mind: the feeling Mr Bennet in *Pride and Prejudice* was experiencing when he dissuaded his daughter from further pianoforte recital by murmuring that she 'had delighted us long enough'.

Though at times transported by Shakespeare she becomes almost wild, there is in Miss Leigh's Cleopatra an arresting streak of Jane Austen. She picks at her part with the daintiness of a debutante called upon to dismember a stag; and her manners are first-rate.

'She plays it' as someone said, 'with her little finger crooked.' This Cleopatra is always civil.

Miss Leigh's piercing candid blankness is superbly pretty, and for several years to come it will not be easy to refrain from wishfully equating her prettiness with greatness. Hers is the magnificent effrontery of an attractive child, endlessly indulged at its first party.

To play Cleopatra the appealing minx must expand and gain texture; and she puts on a low mournful little voice (her first wrinkle) to suggest seediness. But for the outrageous inordinate Queen of Egypt one must return every few seconds to the published version.

Miss Leigh's limitations have wider repercussions than those of most actresses. Sir Laurence with that curious chivalry, which some time or other blights the progress of every great actor, gives me the impression that he subdues his blow-lamp ebullience to match her. Blunting his iron precision, levelling away his towering authority he meets her half-way. Antony climbs down; and Cleopatra pats him on the head. A cat in fact can do more than look at a king: She can hypnotize him. . . .   *Kenneth Tynan, 1951*

RHINOCEROS: Sir Laurence Olivier's performance as Berenger has been widely and justly praised, and one wonders which of its many factors is most beautifully achieved. There is B sly, shiftily eager for drink, B spellbound by the Logician, B humble and eventually B defiant. Sir Laurence plays with fine tact to the impressive people who crowd around him, shout him down, interrupt and disregard him, but he takes hold of the end of the play with a courage and desperation we have watched him build up throughout the evening. Finally in a long pause during which it is barely possible to breathe, his eyes search an auditorium crowded with rhinoceri for a single human face. If for nothing else – and *Rhinoceros* is a play impressive in its mastery of the stage, its handling of purely traditional machinery – we owe M. Ionesco much for providing a part in which Sir Laurence can surprise us with a new dimension of his art.   *The Times, 9 June 1960*

Laurence Olivier as the last exemplar of individualism, is not so much miscast as undercast. Wearing an inexplicable Apache wig, and behaving with a determined kind of boyish hangdog charm, Sir Laurence skitters gracefully around the stage, rolling his eyes and trying hard to seem humble and insignificant. The task is not an easy one, there is never any doubt that with one breath, one vocal blast, one surge of his enormous humanity, he could blow the part to smithereens, and with it the play. He controls himself quite splendidly; one merely laments the waste of his time.

Observer, 12 June 1960

SEMI-DETACHED: It is a dull and silly little play. . . . Heading the cast is Sir Laurence Olivier, our greatest actor. Every now and then he turns a neat bit of business; but that is about all. . . . And if this is the kind of play the Director of the National Theatre thinks worth putting on I can only say that it were better that a Foundation Stone be hanged about his neck and he be cast into the uttermost depths of the sea.

Bernard Levin, Daily Mail, December 1962

UNCLE VANYA (Chichester): . . . the wrong play for the wrong stage. . . . Olivier's unconcentrated production. . . . The entire production came across as runny as an egg too lightly boiled. We saw the play in fragments which never gelled to an emotional whole.

Robert Muller, Daily Mail

This staging is as near perfection as any but a Russian theatre is likely to see and could even, except for the necessity of translation, hold its own against Moscow. Sir Laurence Olivier is the producer who has realized the mounting of the play and he has the support of a faultless cast in which he himself plays Astrov the doctor, while Sir Michael Redgrave plays the title part . . . this production shows the two of them at the very peak of their powers. . . . The balance of the play is beautifully observed. . . . As for the performance of Sir Laurence Olivier, his Astrov is not only the best we are likely to see in our lifetimes but a fresh creation, a kind of revelation of what is in the part. His great scenes, one with Ilyena and one with Vanya, are electrifying. Olivier's production put before us Chekhov in an even more intense, personal light, sometimes, trembling between the pitiful and the farcical, always, ineluctably, right. The whole evening is a memory to cherish.

Tatler, 4 December 1963

OTHELLO: Sensational it is: who would have believed that Sir Laurence could make his voice so deep and dark . . .? The power, passion and verisimilitude of Sir Laurence's performance will be spoken of with wonder for a long time to come.

Harold Hobson, Sunday Times

He came on smelling a rose, laughing softly, with a private delight; barefooted, ankleted, black. He had chosen to play a Negro. . . . It could have been a caricature, an embarrassment. Instead, after the second performance, a well-known Negro actor rose in the stalls bravo-ing. For obviously it was done with love; with the main purpose of substituting for the Moorish empire one modern audiences could respond to: the grandeur of Africa. He was the continent, like a figure of Rubens's allegory. . . . The last speech was spoken kneeling on the bed, her body clutched upright to him as a shield for the dagger he turns on himself. As he *slumped* beside her on the sheets, the current stopped. A couple of wigged actors stood awkwardly about. You could only pity them: we had seen history, and it was over.   *Ronald Bryden, New Statesman*

He came on like Cy Grant – his West Indian accent is totally meaningless. This performance has nothing whatever to do with Othello as Shakespeare wrote it, and remains a great big indigestible lump in the middle of the play. What he gives us is a Notting Hill Gate Negro – a law student from Ghana – and his portrait is made up of all the ludicrous liberal cliché attitudes towards Negroes: beautiful skin, marvellous sense of rhythm, wonderful way of walking, etc. (I believe this wonderful way of walking is in fact limited to a certain type of modern show-biz Negro.) Shakespeare's Othello was a Moor, an Arab, and to emphasize his being *black* in this way makes nonsense of the play.

Jonathan Miller

There is a kind of bad acting of which only a great actor is capable. I find Sir Laurence Olivier's Othello the most prodigious and perverse example of this in a decade. . . . Sir Laurence is elaborately at ease, graceful and suave, more like a seducer than a cuckold. But as the jealousy is transfused into his blood, the white man shows through more obviously. He begins to double and treble his vowels, to stretch his consonants, to stagger and shake, even to vomit, near the frontiers of self-parody. His hips oscillate, his palms rotate, his voice skids and slides so that the Othello music takes on a Beatle beat.   *Alan Brien, Sunday Telegraph*

THE MERCHANT OF VENICE: No one will forget this Shylock's infernal dance of triumph, oddly reminiscent of Hitler at the Arc de Triomphe, when he learns that Antonio's argosy is wrecked. Or his kneeling, broken, to weep at the loss of the turquoise his daughter has stolen. Or at the end, his collapse at the door of the court and – long after he has disappeared – the dreadful off-stage sobbing that at last stirs some sympathy for a man 'baited with the Rabble's curse'.

Unlike some Olivier performances, the studied external detail seems to proceed from the passion within. He has created a man of flint in no way admirable except for his obsessed pride of race.

John Barber, Daily Telegraph, 29 April 1970

Dancing with glee at Antonio's misfortunes, coming to court to cut off the pound of flesh with a briefcase more prominent than a knife, and after sentence apparently falling down stairs off-stage, Sir Laurence will not be remembered for his Shylock. Or if he is, he will be singularly unlucky. *Harold Hobson, Sunday Times*

LONG DAY'S JOURNEY INTO NIGHT: Although Olivier's Tyrone is scaled down to the surrounding company, it is a performance of intense technical and personal fascination. Personal in the sense that James Tyrone was an actor with the kind of career which Olivier has spent his life avoiding: a strong young talent destroyed by years of imprisonment in profitable type casting. We see Tyrone at a stage where he is all too well aware of this; and the dejection that settles on Olivier's frame from the start – his body hunched and his mouth cracked into a small crooked line – expresses a sense of defeat that encompasses the whole of his life and not merely his family. There are touches of the old ham: as where he smugly intones a few of Prospero's lines and turns to his son in naked appeal for applause; and where Olivier pulls out a pair of his own incomparable physical tricks in staging two contrasted descents from a table. But what marks out his performance most from the others is its breadth; all the components of the man are there simultaneously – the tight-wad, the old pro, the distracted husband, the ragged Irish boy – and there is the sense not only that O'Neill is showing off the different sides of the character, but that Olivier is consciously manipulating them for his advantage.

Irving Wardle, The Times, 22 December 1971

As for Sir Laurence Olivier – one of the finest actors in the world playing one of the world's greatest roles – he attacked the elder Tyrone like a character in classical comedy, speaking his lines as if they were verse, and displaying ease only with the miserly side of the character. One had to remember back to the great performance of Fredric March in the original production – self-justifying, raging, mixing reproaches with conciliation and compassion with despair – to recall the torment out of which this part, indeed this whole play, was initially conceived.

Robert Brustein, Observer, 24 December 1972

Theatre Chronology

1916 Brutus in *Julius Caesar* (Shakespeare). Production by All Saints Choir School, Marylebone.

1922 Katharine in *The Taming of the Shrew* (Shakespeare). Production by All Saints Choir School at Stratford Memorial Theatre, Stratford-on-Avon.

1924 Pupil at Elsie Fogerty's Central School of Speech Training and Dramatic Art.

1925 Lennox in *Macbeth* (Shakespeare). Norman V. Norman and Beatrice Wilson's production at the St Christopher Theatre, Letchworth.

Walk-on part as policeman in *The Ghost Train*, also ASM at Brighton Hippodrome.

Series of parts including Flavius in *Julius Caesar* (Shakespeare) with the Lena Ashwell Players at the Century Theatre, Notting Hill Gate, London.

Walk-on part as First Serving Man, also ASM, in *Henry VIII* (Shakespeare) with Sybil Thorndike and Lewis Casson at Empire Theatre, London.

1926 The Minstrel in *The Marvellous History of St Bernard* (Barry Jackson's version of a French mystery play) with the Birmingham Repertory Company at Kingsway Theatre, London.

Minor part in *The Barber and The Cow*, Birmingham Repertory Company's summer season at Clacton.

Richard Coaker in *The Farmer's Wife* (Eden Phillpotts) Birmingham Repertory Company's provincial tour.

Theatre Chronology

1927   Series of parts with the Birmingham Repertory Company under Barry Jackson in Birmingham including Tony Lumpkin in *She Stoops to Conquer* (Goldsmith), title role in *Uncle Vanya* (Chekhov), Monsieur Parolles in *All's Well That Ends Well* (Shakespeare).

1928   Series of parts with the Birmingham Repertory Company
Jan.- at the Royal Court Theatre, London including the Young
May   Man in *The Adding Machine* (Elmer Rice), Malcolm in *Macbeth* (Shakespeare, modern dress), title role in *Harold* (Tennyson), The Lord in *The Taming of the Shrew* (Shakespeare).

June   Gerald Arnwood in *Bird in Hand* (Drinkwater) produced by Barry Jackson with Jill Esmond at Royalty Theatre, London.

Dec.   Stanhope in *Journey's End* (R. C. Sherriff) Stage Society production at Apollo Theatre, London.

1929   Title role in *Beau Geste* (adapted from P. C. Wren's book by Basil Dean) directed by Basil Dean at Her Majesty's Theatre, London.

Mar.   Prince Pao in *The Circle of Chalk* (adapted 'from the ancient Chinese') directed by Basil Dean with Anna May Wong.

April   *Paris Bound* with Herbert Marshall and Edna Best at the Lyric Theatre, London.

June   *The Stranger Within* with Olga Lindo at the Garrick Theatre, London.

Oct.   *Murder on the Second Floor* (Frank Vosper) at the Eltinge Theatre, New York.

Dec.   Jerry Warrender in *The Last Enemy* (Frank Harvey) directed by Tom Walls with Athene Seyler at the Fortune Theatre, London.

1930   Victor Prynne in *Private Lives* (Noël Coward) directed by Noël Coward with Noël Coward and Gertrude Lawrence, at the Phoenix Theatre, London.

1931   *Private Lives* with Noël Coward, Gertrude Lawrence and Jill Esmond at Times Square Theatre, New York.

1933   Stevan Beringer in *The Rats of Norway* (Keith Winter) directed by Raymond Massey with Raymond Massey and Gladys Cooper at the Playhouse Theatre, London.

Julian in *The Green Bay Tree* directed by Jed Harris at the Cort Theatre, New York.

1934   Richard Kurt in *Biography* (S. N. Behrman) directed by Noël Coward with Ina Claire at the Globe Theatre, London.

June   Bothwell in *Queen of Scots* (Gordon Daviot) directed by John Gielgud with Glen Byam Shaw and Campbell Gullan at the New Theatre, London.

Oct.   Tony Cavendish in *Theatre Royal* (Edna Ferber and George Kaufman) directed by Noël Coward with Marie Tempest at the Lyric Theatre, London.

1935   Peter Hammond in *The Ringmaster* (Keith Winter) directed
Mar.   by Raymond Massey with Cathleen Nesbitt and Nigel Patrick at the Shaftesbury Theatre, London.

May   Richard Harben in *Golden Arrow* (Sylvia Thompson and Victor Cunard) presented and directed by Laurence Olivier with Cecil Parker and Greer Garson at the Whitehall Theatre, London.

1935   Romeo in *Romeo and Juliet* (Shakespeare) directed by John
Oct.   Gielgud with Peggy Ashcroft, and John Gielgud as Mercutio at the New Theatre, London. Later switched roles with Gielgud.

1936   Bob Patch in *Bees on the Boatdeck* (J. B. Priestley) presented
May   by Laurence Olivier and Ralph Richardson with Kay Hammond, Rene Ray, Raymond Huntley and Ralph Richardson at the Lyric Theatre, London.

1937   Old Vic Season.
Jan.   Title role in *Hamlet* (Shakespeare) directed by Tyrone Guthrie with Michael Redgrave. Sir Toby Belch in *Twelfth Night* (Shakespeare) directed by Tyrone Guthrie with Jill Esmond. Title role in *Henry V* (Shakespeare) directed by Tyrone Guthrie.

June   Title role in *Hamlet* directed by Tyrone Guthrie with

Vivien Leigh as Ophelia at Kronborg Castle, Elsinore, Denmark.

1937- Second Old Vic Season.
38   Title role in *Macbeth* (Shakespeare) directed by Michael Saint-Denis with Judith Anderson.

Feb. Iago in *Othello* (Shakespeare) directed by Tyrone Guthrie with Ralph Richardson.

Mar. Vivaldi in the *King of Nowhere* (James Bridie) directed by Tyrone Guthrie.

Apr. Title role in *Coriolanus* (Shakespeare) directed by Lewis Casson with Sybil Thorndike.

1939 Gaylord Easterbrook in *No Time For Comedy* (S. N. Behrman) with Katharine Cornell at the Ethel Barrymore Theatre, New York.

1940 Romeo in *Romeo and Juliet* (Shakespeare) directed by Laurence Olivier with Vivien Leigh as Juliet, New York after try-outs in San Francisco and Chicago.

1944 Appointed Co-director of the Old Vic with Ralph Richardson and John Burrell. At New Theatre, London Sergius in *Arms and The Man* (Shaw). The Button Moulder in *Peer Gynt* (Ibsen). Title role in *Richard* III (Shakespeare) directed by John Burrell.

1945 Directed *The Skin of Our Teeth* (Thornton Wilder) with Vivien Leigh at the Phoenix Theatre, London.

Second Old Vic Season at the New Theatre, London.

Jan. Astrov in *Uncle Vanya* (Chekhov). Hotspur in *Henry* IV, *Part One*.

Sept. Justice Shallow in *Henry* IV, *Part Two*.

Oct. Double Bill: Title role in *Oedipus* (Sophocles, translated by W. B. Yeats) and Mr Puff in *The Critic* (Sheridan).
      Arms and The Man, *Peer Gynt* and *Richard* III – Tour of Belgium, Holland, Germany and France playing to army audiences.

1946   *Henry* IV, *Parts One and Two, Oedipus, The Critic,* and *Uncle Vanya* at the Century Theatre, New York, with Old Vic Company.

Sept.   Title role in *King Lear* (Shakespeare) directed by Laurence Olivier at New Theatre, London with Alec Guinness and Old Vic Company.

1947   Received Knighthood 'for services to stage and films'. Presented and directed *Born Yesterday* (Garson Kanin) with Hartley Power and Yolande Donlan at the Garrick Theatre, London.

1948   Tour of Australia and New Zealand with Old Vic Com-
Mar.- pany: Sir Peter Teazle in *The School for Scandal* (Sheridan)
Sept.   directed by Laurence Olivier with Vivien Leigh.

Mr Antrobus in *The Skin of Our Teeth* (Thornton Wilder) directed by Laurence Olivier with Vivien Leigh.

Title role in *Richard* III (Shakespeare) directed by John Burrell.

1949   Old Vic Season at the New Theatre London:
Sir Peter Teazle in *The School for Scandal* (Sheridan) directed by Laurence Olivier with Vivien Leigh.

Chorus in *Antigone* (Anouilh) directed by Laurence Olivier with Vivien Leigh.

Directed *The Proposal* (Chekhov) as curtain-raiser to *Antigone.*

Title role in *Richard* III (Shakespeare) directed by John Burrell.

Oct.   Directed *A Streetcar Named Desire* (Tennessee Williams) with Vivien Leigh, Bonar Colleano, and Bernard Braden at the Aldwych Theatre, London.

Presented *Daphne Laureola* (James Bridie) with Edith Evans at Wyndham's Theatre, London.

1950   Actor-Manager at the St James's Theatre, London:
The Duke of Altair in *Venus Observed* (Christopher Fry) directed by Laurence Olivier with Rachel Kempson, Heather Stannard and Denholm Elliot.

Also presented *Fading Mansion* (Anouilh adapted by Donagh MacDonagh), *Captain Carvallo* (Dennis Cannan), *Top of The Ladder* (Tyrone Guthrie) with John Mills, and *The Consul* (opera by Menotti).

1951 Festival of Britain Productions in association with the Arts Council:

May Caesar in *Caesar and Cleopatra* (Shaw) directed by Michael Benthall with Vivien Leigh.

Antony in *Antony and Cleopatra* (Shakespeare) directed by Michael Benthall with Vivien Leigh.

Oct. Presented Orson Welles in *Othello* (Shakespeare) directed by Orson Welles at the St James's Theatre, London.

Dec. *Caesar and Cleopatra* and *Antony and Cleopatra* at the Ziegfeld Theatre, New York.

1952 Presented Peter Finch in *The Happy Time* (adapted by Samuel Taylor from Robert Fontaine's novel) at the St James's Theatre, London.
Venus Observed at the New Century Theatre, New York.

1953 Presented *Anastasia* (Marcelle Maurette) directed by John
Aug. Counsell at the St James's Theatre, London.

Nov. The Prince in *The Sleeping Prince* (Terence Rattigan) directed by Laurence Olivier at the Phoenix Theatre, London.

1954 Presented *Waiting for Gillian* (adapted by Ronald Millar from Nigel Balchin's novel) directed by Michael Macowan with Frank Lawton, John McCallum and Googie Withers at the St James's Theatre, London.

Presented *Meet A Body* (Frank Launder and Sidney Gilliatt) directed by Henry Kendall with Brian Reece and Patrick Cargill at the Duke of York's Theatre, London.

1955 Season at the Shakespeare Memorial Theatre, Stratford-on-Avon:

Apr. Malvolio in *Twelfth Night* (Shakespeare) directed by John Gielgud with Vivien Leigh.

June   Title role in *Macbeth* (Shakespeare) directed by Glen Byam Shaw with Vivien Leigh.

Aug.   Title role in *Titus Andronicus* (Shakespeare) directed by Peter Brook with Vivien Leigh.

1956   Presented *Double Image* (Roger MacDougall and Ted Allan) with Richard Attenborough at the Savoy Theatre, London.

Presented *Summer of the Seventeenth Doll* (Ray Lawler) directed by Laurence Olivier with Ray Lawler and Madge Ryan at the New Theatre, London.

1957   Archie Rice in *The Entertainer* (John Osborne) directed by Tony Richardson with Brenda de Banzie and Joan Plowright at the Royal Court Theatre, London.

June   *Titus Andronicus*: tour to Paris, Venice, Belgrade, Zagreb, Vienna and Warsaw, and finally at the Stoll Theatre, London.

Sept.   *The Entertainer* transferred to the Palace Theatre, London.

1958   *The Entertainer* at the Royale Theatre, New York.

1959   Title role in *Coriolanus* (Shakespeare) directed by Peter Hall at Shakespeare Memorial Theatre, Stratford-on-Avon.

1960   Berenger in *Rhinoceros* (Ionesco) directed by Orson Welles
Apr.   at the Royal Court Theatre, London.

Oct.   Becket in *Becket* (Anouilh) directed by Peter Glenville with Anthony Quinn as King Henry at St James's Theatre, New York. Later took over role of Henry when Quinn left the cast.

1961   Appointed Director of Chichester Festival Theatre.
Directed *The Chances* (John Fletcher).

Prologue and Bassanes in *The Broken Heart* (John Ford) directed by Laurence Olivier.

Astrov in *Uncle Vanya* (Chekhov) directed by Laurence Olivier.

Dec.   Fred Midway in *Semi-Detached* (David Turner) directed by Tony Richardson at the Saville Theatre, London.

1963   Appointed Director of the National Theatre.

Oct.   Directed *Hamlet* (Shakespeare) with Peter O'Toole, Rosemary Harris, Michael Redgrave and Max Adrian. Inaugural Production of the National Theatre at the Old Vic.

Astrov in *Uncle Vanya* (Chekhov) directed by Laurence Olivier at the National (Old Vic).

Captain Brazen in *The Recruiting Officer* (Farquhar) directed by William Gaskill at the National Theatre (Old Vic).

1964   Title role in *Othello* (Shakespeare) directed by John Dexter
Apr.   with Maggie Smith and Frank Finlay at the National Theatre (Old Vic).

Solness in *The Master Builder* (Ibsen) directed by Peter Wood with Joan Plowright at the National Theatre (Old Vic).

1965   Directed *The Crucible* (Arthur Miller) with Colin Blakeley and Joyce Redman at the National Theatre (Old Vic).

Tattle in *Love for Love* (Congreve) directed by Peter Wood and title role in *Othello* – National Theatre tour to Berlin and Moscow.

Oct.   Tattle in *Love for Love*, with John Stride and Geraldine McEwan at the National Theatre (Old Vic).

1967

Feb.   Edgar in *The Dance of Death* (Strindberg) directed by Glen Byam Shaw with Geraldine McEwan at the National Theatre (Old Vic).

Plucheux in *A Flea in Her Ear* (Feydeau) at the National Theatre (Old Vic).

Directed *Three Sisters* (Chekhov) with Joan Plowright at the National Theatre (Old Vic).

The Dance of Death, Love for Love, and *A Flea in Her Ear* – Canadian Tour with National Theatre Company.

1968   Directed *Love's Labour Lost* (Shakespeare) at National Theatre (Old Vic).

Co-directed with Donald MacKechnie *The Advertisement*

(Natalia Ginzburg) with Joan Plowright at the National (Old Vic).

1970   Created Baron Olivier in the Birthday Honours List.

Apr.   Shylock in *The Merchant of Venice* (Shakespeare) directed by Jonathan Miller with Joan Plowright. at the National Theatre (Old Vic).

1971   Directed *Amphitryon 38* (Giraudoux) with Christopher
June   Plummer, Geraldine McEwan and National Theatre Company at the New Theatre, London.

Dec.   James Tyrone in *Long Day's Journey Into Night* (Eugene O'Neill) directed by Michael Blakemore with Constance Cummings and National Theatre Company at the New Theatre, London.

1972   *Long Day's Journey Into Night* at the National Theatre (Old Vic).

Film Chronology

1930 The Man in *Too Many Crooks* (UK) directed by George King with Dorothy Boyd and A. Bromley Davenport.

Peter Bille in *The Temporary Widow* (UK, Germany) directed by Gustav Ucicky with Lilian Harvey and Felix Aylmer.

1931 Lieutenant Nichols in *Friends and Lovers* (USA) directed by Victor Schertzinger with Adolphe Menjou and Eric von Stroheim.

Straker in *Potiphar's Wife* (UK) directed by Maurice Elvey with Nora Swinburne and Norman McKinnel. (US title: *Her Strange Desire*.)

Julian Rolphe in *The Yellow Passport* (USA) directed by Raoul Walsh with Elissa Landi and Lionel Barrymore. (USA title: *The Yellow Ticket*.)

1932 Nick Allen in *Westward Passage* (USA) directed by Robert Milton with Ann Harding and Zasu Pitts.

1933 Clive in *No Funny Business* (UK) directed by John Stafford and Victor Hanbury with Gertrude Lawrence and Jill Esmond.

Nicholas Randall in *Perfect Understanding* (UK) directed by Cyril Gardner with Gloria Swanson and John Halliday.

1935 Ignatov in *Moscow Nights* (UK) directed by Anthony Asquith with Harry Baur and Penelope Ward.

1936 Orlando in *As You Like It* (UK) directed by Paul Czinner with Elisabeth Bergner and Leon Quartermaine.

Vincent Lunardi in *Conquest of the Air* (UK) directed by Alexander Korda with Hay Petrie and Franklyn Dyall.

1937 Larry Durrant in *Twenty One Days* (UK) (Original title *The First and The Last*) directed by Basil Dean with Vivien Leigh and Leslie Banks. (USA title: *Twenty One Days Together*.)

Michael Ingalby in *Fire Over England* (UK) directed by William K. Howard with Flora Robson and Vivien Leigh.

1938 Logan in *The Divorce of Lady X* (UK) directed by Tim Whelan with Merle Oberon and Ralph Richardson.

1939 Heathcliff in *Wuthering Heights* (USA) directed by William Wyler with Merle Oberon and David Niven.

Tony McVane in *Q Planes* (UK) directed by Tim Whelan with Valerie Hobson and Ralph Richardson. (USA title: *Clouds over Europe*.)

1940 D'Arcy in *Pride and Prejudice* (USA) directed by Robert K. Leonard with Greer Garson and Maureen O'Sullivan.

Max de Winter in *Rebecca* (USA) directed by Alfred Hitchcock with Joan Fontaine and George Sanders.

1941 Lord Nelson in *Lady Hamilton* (USA) directed by Alexander Korda with Vivien Leigh and Sara Allgood. (USA title: *That Hamilton Woman*.)

Johnnie in *49th Parallel* (UK) directed by Michael Powell with Leslie Howard and Raymond Massey. (USA title: *The Invaders*.)

1943 Ivan Kouznetsoff in *The Demi-Paradise* (UK) directed by Anthony Asquith with Penelope Ward and Margaret Rutherford. (USA title: *Adventure for Two*.)

1945 Title role in *Henry v* (UK) directed by Laurence Olivier (and Richard Beck) with Renée Asherson and Leslie Banks.

1948 Title role in *Hamlet* (UK) directed by Laurence Olivier with Jean Simmons and Felix Aylmer.

1951 George Hurstwood in *Carrie* (USA) directed by William Wyler with Jennifer Jones and Miriam Hopkins.

Cameo role as policeman PC 94 B in *The Magic Box* (UK) directed by John Boulting with Maria Schell and Robert Donat.

Film Chronology

1953   MacHeath in *The Beggars' Opera* (UK) directed by Peter Brook, co-produced by Laurence Olivier and Herbert Wilcox with Dorothy Tutin and Stanley Holloway.

1955   Title role in *Richard III* (UK) directed by Laurence Olivier and Anthony Bushell with Claire Bloom, Ralph Richardson and John Gielgud.

1957   Grand Duke Charles in *The Prince and the Showgirl* (UK) directed by Laurence Olivier with Marilyn Monroe and Sybil Thorndike.

1959   General Burgoyne in *The Devil's Disciple* (UK) directed by Guy Hamilton with Burt Lancaster and Kirk Douglas.

1960   Crassus in *Spartacus* (USA) directed by Stanley Kubrick with Jean Simmons and Kirk Douglas.

Archie Rice in *The Entertainer* (UK) directed by Tony Richardson with Joan Plowright and Albert Finney.

1962   Graham Weir in *Term of Trial* (UK) directed by Peter Glenville with Simone Signoret and Terence Stamp.

1965   Newhouse in *Bunny Lake is Missing* (UK) directed by Otto Preminger with Carol Lynley and Noël Coward.

Title role in *Othello* (UK) directed by Stuart Burge with Maggie Smith and Frank Finlay.

1966   The Mahdi in *Khartoum* (UK) directed by Basil Dearden with Charlton Heston and Ralph Richardson.

1968   Edgar in *The Dance of Death* (UK) directed by David Giles with Geraldine McEwan and Robert Lang.

Premier Kamenev in *The Shoes of the Fisherman* (USA) directed by Michael Anderson with Anthony Quinn and Oskar Werner.

1969   Creakle in *David Copperfield* (UK) directed by Delbert Mann with Robin Phillips, Edith Evans and Ralph Richardson.

Air Chief Marshal Sir Hugh Dowding in *The Battle of Britain* (UK) directed by Guy Hamilton with Michael Caine and Michael Redgrave.

Field-Marshal Sir John French in *Oh! What a Lovely War*

(UK) directed by Richard Attenborough with all-star cast including John Gielgud and Ralph Richardson.

1970   Doctor Chebutikin in *Three Sisters* (UK) directed by Laurence Olivier with Joan Plowright and Alan Bates.

1971   Count Witte in *Nicholas and Alexander* (USA) directed by Franklin Schaffner with Janet Suzman and Harry Andrews.

1972   Wellington in *Lady Caroline Lamb* (UK) directed by Robert Bolt with Sarah Miles and Richard Chamberlain.

Andrew Wyke in *Sleuth* (UK) directed by Joseph L. Mankiewicz with Michael Caine and Alec Cawthorne.

Photographic Acknowledgements

Angus McBean (Harvard Theatre Collection): 3, 4, 5, 6, 14, 15, 17, 19, 20, 22, 23, 24, 25, 28, jacket back. Anthony Crickmay: 31. Associated Newspapers: 16. Associated Press Photographs: 18. British Lion: 21. Camera Press: 30, 32 (Sophie Baker). John Vickers: 8, 9, 11, 12, 13. National Film Archive: 1, 7. Paramount Pictures: 29. Radio Times Hulton Picture Library: 2, 10. *Sunday Times Magazine*: 34 (Brian Morris). Twentieth Century Fox: 33. Zoe Dominic: 26, 27, jacket front.